Praise for *Parental Control*

"Given the failure of Big Tech to provide appropriate guardrails to keep our kids safe online, it is up to us. We must be their 'parental controls,' which takes education, communication, and an open heart. Titania skillfully guides parents through this unprecedented time in *Parental Control*."

—Nicki Reisberg
Host of Scrolling 2 Death *podcast*

"*Parental Control* by Titania Jordan is an essential guide for parents navigating the complexities of raising children in this new age of social media. With inspiring courage, Ms. Jordan shares her personal experiences, offering invaluable insights into some of the severe social media-related risks and challenges that threaten our children while also destigmatizing some essential safety conversations for families. *Parental Control* provides practical strategies for maximizing safety and fostering open, supportive communication between parents and children. As the CEO of the Organization for Social Media Safety, I know firsthand how vital this advice is for parents seeking to protect and empower their children, and Ms. Jordan's contributions have added much-needed clarity to the ongoing social media safety conversation. This book is a must-read for any parent committed to raising kids safely in today's social media age."

—Marc Berkman
CEO of Organization for Social Media Safety

"During a time when online safety is a universal concern for all parents, Titania Jordan delivers a must-have resource for every home. Timely, powerful, and a must-read for families today."

—Rania Mankarious (MA, JD)
CEO of Crime Stoppers of Houston and author of
The Online World: What You Think You Know and What You Don't

"Most guidance on social media, technology, and children just causes parents to worry and feel helpless. *Parental Control* is different, delivered in a fact-based and empathetic way that only Titania Jordan—with her years of experience in this topic—can. *Parental Control* empowers parents with clear, evidence-based, and truly boots-on-the-ground actionable recommendations that restore a healthy perspective to our use of technology, put parents back in the driver seat, and allow our children to thrive."

—Dr. Darria Long

National bestselling author of Mom Hacks, *founder of No-Panic Parenting, and clinical assistant professor at the University of Tennessee School of Health Sciences*

"Everyone is talking about tech problems. But with Titania, we have a wise, passionate, and loving mom, who pours out the practical path forward we so desperately need."

—Chris McKenna

Founder, Protect Young Eyes

Parental
Control

Parental Control

A Guide to Raising Balanced Kids in the Digital Era

Titania Jordan

JB JOSSEY-BASS™
A Wiley Brand

Published by John Wiley & Sons, Inc., Hoboken, New Jersey.
Published simultaneously in Canada.

ISBNs: 9781394256556 (Hardback), 9781394256570 (ePDF), 9781394256563 (ePub).

For general information on our other products and services or for technical support, please contact our Customer Care Department within the United States at (800) 762-2974, outside the United States at (317) 572-3993 or fax (317) 572-4002.

Wiley also publishes its books in a variety of electronic formats. Some content that appears in print may not be available in electronic formats. For more information about Wiley products, visit our web site at www.wiley.com.

Library of Congress Control Number: 2024053833 (print)

Cover Design: Wiley
Cover Image: © pedrorsfernandes/Shutterstock
Author Photo: © Kate Blohm

SKY10096863_012225

For every parent who realizes that no parenting book can fully prepare you for your unique journey with your unique child. If your child knows they are loved unconditionally, you have already won in the long-run.

For Brian Bason and Brandon Hilkert, two incredible dads who started a company that saves children's lives daily and entrusted me to tell our story.

For Matt McKee who left this planet too soon and truly made a difference.

Contents

Introduction

Let's start this off with a thank you. Just by picking up this book, you have taken the hardest and most necessary step—realizing you might need help dealing with the challenges of the digital age.

Before taking any sort of action to course-correct or lean into the intuition that you might be on the wrong path, you've stopped and reached out. Good for you.

Chances are, you have participated in multiple conversations with your children, partner, teachers, or other parents about how much has changed with the advent of the digital age.

When you have those conversations, there's a collective agreement that, yes, there is a big problem, but then those conversations inevitably trail off with a shrug, no solutions, and a general feeling of helplessness—what can we do?

The name of this book, *Parental Control*, was suggested to me by my publisher in a true lightbulb moment that I immediately gravitated toward. The previous working title, *Playgrounds to Pixels*, didn't hit hard enough and wasn't keying in on what most parents are lacking today.

Parental. Control.

In other words, this book offers clear relational and technical guidelines for how to raise children in a world that gives them unprecedented access (to adult content and strangers) before they are mature enough to handle what that kind of access brings.

Parents need to be empowered to be the parent.

Since the advent of parenting, parents have historically set healthy boundaries for their children in all areas of their development, and yet parents over the past 20 years have lost more of their ability to set those boundaries than ever before due to technology and social media.

In a sense, while children are now growing up and processing information faster than ever before, parents across the globe are simultaneously regressing.

As a result, what we are seeing is that both children and their parents are no longer thriving but surviving.

The answer is not to revert to the time when children were seen and not heard.

I hope you can quickly gather by reading this book that the title *Parental Control* is not a heavy-handed, authoritarian, disciplinarian ode to the old-school style of parenting.

It's meant to be slightly ironic given how little we actually can control in life.

It's meant to put things in perspective for you: how to control what you can control with a healthy balance of grace, education, and empowerment.

The end goal of this book is to help your child experience a relatively unscathed childhood (at least when it comes to technology) because you, their parent or caregiver, is equipped with the right knowledge and perspective to navigate this rocky landscape.

You are not meant to remove every boulder from your child's path.

You are responsible, however, for having the wisdom to anticipate the obstacles your child might face in this new landscape of childhood and discuss those situations with them well in advance of them actually taking place.

Much like you place a toddler in a car seat to protect them from:

- climbing all around the inside of car while it's in motion,
- others on the road,
- a car accident,

you need those same kinds of tools for your child's digital world.

You also need tips for how to manage and build a solid relationship with your child in a world that we (and our grandparents and our great-grandparents) did not grow up in.

In this book I turn to the experts frequently to help me help you, and it's through this collective mindshare that we will emerge triumphant. I also share personal experiences from my life to add context to how I landed where I have.

Most of the resources and data available acknowledge that there is a problem with screens, the Internet, social media, and technology in general as they relate to children. If you stop your scroll or watch the news, you might even see a huge bright spotlight on it, in fact.

But the solutions? Few and far between.

That's where this book comes in, and that's why I was just congratulating you for picking it up. That's the first step. And you can't begin a journey without taking that first step.

Along this journey, you aren't going to get everything right, and that's okay. However, the one thing we *can't* do is nothing.

Education is going to be our most helpful tool moving forward, which is what I hope to offer you.

We're all struggling with living with tiny supercomputers in our pockets. As media consumption has evolved from newspapers to radio to televisions to smartphones—we've had to adapt how we evaluate what we are consuming and how we best filter that information so it doesn't overwhelm, harm, or misinform our children.

Outside of a few pioneers, therapists, researchers, scientists, and doctors, the playbook for how to do this now was largely unscripted. As Joel Stoddard, MD, MAS, at Children's Hospital Colorado says in the documentary *Childhood 2.0*, "Right now we're effectively living in an experiment. How is this going to affect us? We'll find out."

We don't know what we don't know, and that was a somewhat acceptable excuse when smartphones and social media first launched.

But, we have enough information now.

We—adults, parents, caregivers, lawmakers, educators, healthcare professionals, tech executives—have to step up.

So What Am I Doing About It?

Things really ramped up when I joined Bark Technologies. You'll hear more about that in a bit. I started the Parenting in a Tech World Facebook Group in 2017 and co-authored *Parenting in a Tech World* in 2020 with Matt McKee.

It was an easy and reasonable entrance into this publishing world thanks to the support of our team at Bark. Shameless plug, but I'd suggest folks pick this up to gain some additional insight and hear directly from an amazing human who is no longer on this planet.

As an aside, Matt passed away in July 2023, and I think of him often, working hard to try to make him proud and carry on the work he so passionately pursued. He wanted to make a difference, and he absolutely did. His email signature didn't tout his professional accomplishments as an investor and entrepreneur but said "just a guy trying to make a difference." He was good and faithful (for those of you who recognize this, Matthew 25:23). He was an incredible dad, husband, friend, and colleague. He is sorely missed.

And now? I'm working on this book. I'm speaking to parents, media outlets, and educators across the globe to share with them what I've learned (both professionally and personally as the mom of a teenager). I'm working furiously to use my social media platforms for good—to essentially do no harm in a place rife with harm. I am sharing my personal stories to bring the perspective of an adult who is part of the last generation to have a childhood (mostly) free of digital dangers.

My Journey

Speaking of wanting to reveal one's true purpose and making sense of pain, here is some perspective I can bring to this book nine years after joining a tech company that helps to protect over 7 million children across the nation and five years after publishing *Parenting in a Tech World* where—since then—we've seen:

- An unprecedented global pandemic
- A ridiculously addictive app called TikTok dominate our children's attention spans and potentially get banned from the United States
- Multiple social justice movements and campus protests
- Two heated, Twitter-tirade strewn, presidential elections
- Heads of the largest global social media companies testifying before the U.S. Congress
- U.S. Surgeon General warnings issued around the dangers of social media and the stressful state of parenting

And so much more.

Additionally, I draw upon my own childhood, teenage and college years, early adulthood, motherhood, and career experiences as they uniquely position me to speak to all of this. I certainly didn't know what I was being prepared for at the time, but I'm grateful for all of it—even the most painful of times.

I am a survivor of childhood sexual abuse, but during a time where the abuser had to be in the same room as me. I discuss this more in Chapter 1.

I struggled with eating disorders and body image issues from a young age—without the help of influential algorithms to push me further and faster down those unhealthy paths.

I experimented sexually and with substances in my risk-taking, endorphin-seeking, acceptance-craving youth, but thankfully those choices were not captured on anything but perhaps one of those yellow and black disposable cameras.

I felt the very real fear of not wanting to be on this planet anymore if the pain didn't go away, but before a time when we had a suicide hotline to call (the number is 988 by the way) and more people publicly and unabashedly saying *it's ok to not be ok*. I share my terrifying experience with suicidal ideation in Chapter 3.

My loving, attentive, kind, hardworking, and caring parents missed most of this back in the 80s and 90s and 00s when I was growing up (through no fault of their own). But similar parents are missing this even more now.

Our kids are struggling.

Good kids. Your kids. My kid.

I can't go back in time and make different choices, but I can acknowledge them, learn from them, and share them with you right here in this book to help you avoid those same mistakes. It's all about your kids from here forward. You and me? We are doing this for them.

These collective experiences in an analog world that eventually turned digital helped shape my decision to write this. My DMs are blowing up. My email inbox will most likely never get to zero again. The questions in the Parenting in a Tech World Facebook Group keep coming.

From church congregations to PTA meetings to student assemblies to book clubs to literally anywhere parents or students congregate, they ask me to share what I know and what we can do about it—and it continues to humble and inspire me.

But it takes people like me, who can move from "why me" to "why not me" to do great things on this planet.

I can't tell you how many times I've been in an important meeting or in the middle of a live television interview, and while appearing calm and collected externally, I have just been frozen internally.

My internal dialogue sounding something like, "Oh my gosh! If they really could see inside my head right now and know what my abilities aren't, they'd ask me to leave. How am I even here? Why am I here, of all people, right now? And when will my heart stop beating out of my chest and my knees stop shaking uncontrollably?"

Then I read the book *Lean In* by Sheryl Sandberg. It was gifted to me by a former CEO I worked with, and I will be forever grateful for his gift. Upon learning that she held executive positions at Google and later Facebook and she still suffered from imposter syndrome, I was like, "Hold up. No. That's crazy. That is absolutely crazy." And suddenly a great veil was lifted.

So knowing that everybody that you encounter, at some point, struggles with feeling like they're not good enough, they're not smart enough, they're not fast enough, or they're not innovative enough, helps you to realize that, "You know what? I'm okay. I'm great actually. I'm going to have good days. I'm going to have bad days. But I'm just as capable as the next person of doing unimaginable things."

So as objectively as possible, I looked at where I was in my life: the mother of a teenage boy, an aunt to four, the wife of a fellow Millennial, the daughter of two Boomer parents, the friend to other people—fellow moms, dads, and dog-moms and cat-dads.

I acknowledged that I was (and still am) the chief parenting officer and chief marketing officer of Bark Technologies, a company that helps protect more than 7 million children across the nation and launched a first-of-its-kind safer smartphone and smart watch for kids.

I have contributed to almost every major media outlet about this topic, and I have been processing multiple Google Alerts daily for the past decade around terms like "parental controls" and "teens and social media" and "digital parenting" and so much more.

Those are the facts. And I didn't choose the "parenting in a tech world" life, the parenting in a tech world life chose me. With great power comes great responsibility, right?

I'll never forget speaking at a local Atlanta prestigious private school (encompassing newborns to 12 grade) in 2018 and having the middle school principal tell me, "Titania, sexting is the new first base."

That will never leave me. I was floored.

This whole thing started slow. I first started gathering my old presentations, iPhone notes, thousands of screenshots on my camera roll, and, yes, pages and pages of old-school notebook paper where I had started writing bits and pieces of what I thought the world wanted to hear. And here I am. Verified badges across social media and all. Not that that means anything—especially because you can now buy them—but it also kind of does for the purposes of this book.

What do I want for you? What is my hope? The purpose of this book is to give you the knowledge and strategies you need to parent in a world that has never existed before, with balance. I want to help you create a reasonable plan of action for your children, household, and community so the later elementary and middle school years don't take you by surprise and fill you with regret. I want more children to have a childhood that's safe. Grounded, insightful, educated, social, loving, wholesome, authentic, connected within reason…and safe.

My wish is providing something that I wasn't provided. Arming more parents or just people around children with a true guidebook and go-to aid for trying to raise well-adjusted children in a world brimming with bytes and pixels. Ultimately, I want you to equip yourself with the know-how and toolkit to usher the next generation into an adulthood where technology still complements, but not consumes, their lives.

So here's what you can expect as you dig into this book. (I'm all about clarity and managing expectations). First, I'm going to give you some background on me—where I come from, how I got here, and why I'm so passionate about keeping kids safer online. Ideally, I'll answer some of the questions around why you should give a rip about what I have to say and why the perfect time for you to be reading this book is right now.

Hint: We now have more science to verify what our gut has been telling us, but it's still early enough to create changes that make a lasting impact.

As a survivor of childhood sexual abuse, I'm passionate about educating and empowering the general public on just how frequently it happens and how you can help your child avoid falling into those same spaces and experiences. I've also struggled with and overcome disordered eating and suicidal ideation. Again, I did that in a time and space where I didn't have an algorithm that could potentially further influence me into deeper and darker spaces.

Being a mother, having lived through all of that, and having seen the before (analog) and after (digital), it's so heartbreaking to know how many parents have no idea that their children are struggling. And it's gut wrenching to know how many children are struggling and don't feel like they can go to their parents or caregivers to get the help they need.

We will also take a look at the analog era when life looked like an OG Instagram filter (and most of the people who work at Instagram were just twinkles in their parents' eyes) and sit with the critical components of what made that time so unique. So much of what transferred into our early digital experiences came as a result of what we experienced during the pre-digital, or analog age.

Nostalgia is a very powerful thing.

As our slow childhoods were followed by a rapid digital transformation—we are now on the other side of it (er, in the middle of it? Does it ever have an end?)—and we can see more clearly how the tools and tech radically changed our lives, childhood, and parenting uniquely and specifically, and begin to see our children's future through a clearer lens.

You know how once you learn something profound, you can never go back? Take Jimi Hendrix's classic "Purple Haze" for example. Instead of singing, "Excuse me while I kiss the sky," some people heard, "Excuse me while I kiss this guy." Once I heard the actual correct lyrics, the entire song made much more sense to me. Well, that's exactly what I'm going to try to do in this book.

I am going to highlight what we know to be true so we can make better decisions.

Some of it will be hard.

Some of it will be heavy.

All of it will help you become the best parent possible given the current unprecedented circumstances.

We'll take a look at where we currently stand and examine the effects this modern, constantly connected technology has on our brains, our bodies, and our minds.

My goal is to provide a guidebook with realistic answers and helpful suggestions on what you can do to parent better in the midst of this technological onslaught.

With *Parental Control* I will outline the many tangible and impactful things you can do because, remember, it's not about me showing up and freaking you out and then peacing out; it's about me educating and empowering you to be the best parent, grandparent, caregiver, aunt, uncle, older sibling, or educator possible.

All of my recommendations come to you from both a professional and a personal place.

Use what works for you and let me know what you found useful if you feel so inclined. My contact information can be found at the very back of this book or in the audiobook notes if you are listening to this.

As Jonathan Haidt wrote in his book *The Anxious Generation*, "Overprotection in the real world and underprotection in the virtual world—are the major reasons why children born after 1995 became the anxious generation." I aim to help your children be better protected in the virtual world, and I just don't know if I believe we can "overprotect" anyone who might be vulnerable anywhere. And I'll be blunt, our children are vulnerable everywhere.

After we cover what you can say and do to have optimal "parental control"—I'll aim to provide my perspective around both what will likely happen if the majority of us do *not* take heed of what is presented in this book and, conversely, what will ideally happen if we take action collectively for the good of this and future generations.

As Gordon Neufeld, PhD, and Gabor Maté, PhD, wrote in their book *Hold Onto Your Kids: Why Parents Matter More Than Peers,* "Our society does not serve the developmental needs of our children." I'd imagine that the influx of screens and technology has only propagated this disservice.

Parents often resign to allowing far too much technology to factor into their children's lives. And who can blame them? They are so ridiculously busy themselves. Screens are simultaneously the best and worst babysitters. Online, not only do children find a way to stay busy, but in many cases, they develop ways to communicate and build friendships.

Unfortunately, these children find themselves in, as Neufeld and Maté wrote, "attachment voids everywhere, and situations in which they lack consistent and deep connection with nurturing adults." How often are adults even in the room when our children are gaming or scrolling or taking selfies?

The authors continue: "Older generations have often in the past complained about the young being less respectful and less disciplined than they used to be, but today many parents intuitively know that something is amiss."

In other words, we know in our guts and in our souls all this technology just isn't right—that simply letting our kids figure it all out by themselves really isn't the route here. Nor do we have the luxury of waiting on legislation to pass or big tech to course correct.

But why is it that, as the book states, "They (children) appear to be easily bored when away from each other or when not engaged with technology. Creative, solitary play seems a vestige of the past."

We can name so many problems that children face today that we may have experienced, but on such a lesser degree. From the house to school to any place we gather, the challenges for the youth seem to continue to mount, and the solutions seemingly more convoluted and complex.

Self-control is an issue. There's drug use, violence, overall malaise, self-harm, and suicide. Those teaching and educating say their jobs are growing harder, that children today just aren't the same. There was even a *Saturday Night Live* skit recently titled "Teacher PSA" with the cast repeatedly stating "Y'all won" when referencing the out-of-control behavior of students this year. Not only was it hilarious, but it was painfully accurate.

And we have seen so many adults go to doctors to find help for their children—or any sort of answers—often resulting in a staggering number of kids and teens with prescriptions for some sort of psychotropic drug designed to address diagnosis of depression, anxiety, bipolar disorder, ADHD, restless leg syndrome (RLS), and a host of other diagnoses when we (perhaps) haven't fully examined the physiological changes that could be made to help mitigate those symptoms (like more recess and less sitting).

Speaking of our search for answers, toward the end of this book, there's a question/answer section that speaks directly and bluntly about the pervasive issues plaguing parents today. I'll answer the most frequently asked questions I receive from parents and caregivers just like you.

I've also gathered a glossary of terms, including emoji and slang meanings, that will provide you with more insight into the tech language kids are speaking and most certainly will make you feel old. You're welcome. As an aside, using any of these with your older children and gauging their reaction is a great way to bond, even if they think you are completely *cheugy* (see Chapter 11 if you don't know what that means).

So, are you ready to dive deep? I'm already there. Join me. I'll hold your hand and provide you with oxygen through the entire process.

1

Why Me, Why Now?

This chapter may or may not be relevant to you—and if you picked up this book to get straight to the "what do I do?" part of how to parent in a tech world, that's totally fine, and you might want to skip this chapter. My ego will not be offended.

If you do, however, want to get to know my *why* behind what I do and how I got to be where I am today, then these next few pages will support your quest in understanding me and my perspective.

The Short Version

I am part of the only and last generation to straddle the pre-social media and post-social media world.

I'm a mother.

I'm a survivor.

I've worked in the parenting/media/tech spaces for more than 20 years.

Over the past nine years alone I've served as the chief parent officer and chief marketing officer for Bark Technologies, an online safety company that helps protect more than seven million children across the United States, Australia, South Africa, and Guam.

I was born into an analog (noncomputerized) household with a childhood full of books and play like the generations who came before me.

I grew up experiencing a rapid technological evolution with connected tech, the Internet, and social media while I was actually "mature" enough to process and utilize it.

I was given incredible, unique opportunities to discuss these issues with experts much smarter than I across global platforms.

I've coached Drew Barrymore on how to keep kids safer online, I've covered teen texting and emoji slang with Steve Harvey, I've surfaced dangers of Snapchat to *Good Morning America*, and I've testified before legislators around the rate at which children are harmed online given our data at Bark. I've spoken with countless numbers of parents whose children have been harmed by unfettered and unmonitored access to tech, and I've been told I have a unique way of helping overwhelmed parents navigate this new parenting landscape with grace given my upbringing and experience.

My purpose on this planet is to help others. I sincerely hope this helps you.

The Long Version

All right, buckle up, here comes the longer story.

So, who am I? Well, my name is Titania Jordan. That's pronounced like the name Tanya or Tonya—and then stutter the T. Now try it out loud. Much easier, right?

Side note—I wish current Titania could go back and tell child Titania that her name is the coolest and it turns out the more unique your name is, the easier it will be to grab social media handles.

But back to the point: who is Titania Jordan, and why should I listen to her?

Good questions. Let's start with the first.

I'm going to go ahead and take you back to the beginning, like the actual beginning.

The Last True Childhood

I was born at the start of the awesome 80s in Tazewell, a very small town in the heart of Appalachia and the coal mining mountains of Virginia. And yes, *that* Tazewell—the one that gained fame in the March 2005 issue of *Time Magazine*[1] for its OxyContin problem.

That's not how I remember it, though. Back then, it was bucolic in every sense of the term. Pleasant elements of country life appeared everywhere you looked, and if my memory serves me as well as a five-year-old's memory can, it was truly breathtaking.

Tazewell offered rolling hills and snowy fields and horses and wild-flowers and unlocked doors and small-town church vibes and all that jazz. I'll never forget the taste of my first donut—it was glazed and in-freaking-credible. I've never had a donut that good and am confident I never will again. Many thanks to the church lady at the local (only) Baptist Church who opened my eyes to that baked goodness.

My father was a business-savvy, handy guy, and my mother was a "couldn't-hurt-a-fly" nurse. She, to this day, still ushers bugs out of the house gently on paper instead of crushing them with a shoe or swatter because…they have feelings and a family too.

A few rad years later, my younger sister came along. Apparently, I was incredibly jealous of her out of the womb—but funny enough, today she is now my best friend. We lived in a pretty incredible two-story colonial brick house that my dad built, and I attended the local public school (I think there was only one in the entire town) where I vividly remember watching *Sesame Street* as a group activity on a TV that rolled in on wheels, pretending to sleep during nap time, watching the mischievous kids get spankings for acting up, and spending lots *and lots* of time outside.

We had one television in our home with fewer than 30 channels of content to choose from, and the only things I watched on it were educational children's programming and MTV at night with my dad back when MTV was literally only music videos. We share a deep love of great music to this day.

I colored, played outside a lot, played with toys, and played with friends. My one best friend, a boy whose dad was the town pediatrician, had a massive Victorian house and cable TV. We watched shows like *He-Man* and *She-Ra*, which I most likely wouldn't have been allowed to watch at my house given the themes of magic and dark forces.

It's funny when I think back on the parental controls my parents had in their toolbelt.

(That means not many.)

But letting my sister and I know that we were not going to be a house where magic and dark forces were allowed clued me in to our household boundaries. So what did we do when we couldn't scratch that proverbial pop culture itch?

We just went next door! The fact that we weren't allowed to watch certain programs or play certain games or read certain books but our friends could meant that, well, we'd just go over to our friends' houses, right? Does this sound familiar with phones or video games or other media where you set a limit and someone else allows it?

Despite how it took place so long ago, it reminds me of a recent quote from a dear friend of mine, the founder of Protect Young Eyes, Chris McKenna. "Our children are only as safe as their friend with the weakest digital rules."

A few years later, my family moved from the tiny town of Tazewell to the big city of Atlanta, Georgia, when my dad got a new job. Let me just say that culture shock is real. Despite my young age, I knew things were different now. Much different.

We found a significantly smaller, one-story rental home, and my sister and I were enrolled in St. Martin's, a small private Episcopalian school. This must've been when I was around five or six years old. I noticed way fewer kids in my new class and a stronger emphasis on art and music. I absolutely loved it and attended pre-K through 8th grade at that beloved school.

Our Atlanta honeymoon was short-lived. Like so many marriages in the 1980s, my parents divorced shortly after the boxes were unpacked. Jackie (my sister) and I were still very young, and somehow, we understood that we were fiercely loved by both our parents. Despite the rift from our parents splitting, we still knew that everything was going to be okay. In retrospect, my parents weren't really the most compatible couple, so it was probably (ultimately) best for both of them. But this was a big event in my life. It still is. Not necessarily a negative. But impactful.

In our new setup following the divorce, in a two-bedroom, two-bathroom Buckhead apartment while with my mom (majority of the time) and a variety of nearby places while with my dad (every other weekend), we had only one television (in both homes) with just the basic channels. In fact, we had to literally turn a knob on the TV to change the channel or adjust the volume. At first, I think there were 3 channels, and then there were, like, 12 channels. And then cable came along, and there were a lot more. And then there was the Internet.

But today the media landscape is like taking a glass globe, shattering it, and all those pieces of glass are the fragments now with which you have to get people's attention.

And that's not just a TV screen. It's mobile devices. It's an iPad. It's everywhere.

Everybody's competing for everyone's attention, all the time. I mean, there are screens at the gas station now and screens built into the backs of seat headrests in luxury vehicles. Everywhere you look, screens large and small are competing for your attention.

I guess that's one of the reasons I enjoy branding, design, and copyrighting—because you have to constantly be going to the next level to figure out how to capture somebody's attention as there's such a fight for it. The competition for your eyeballs is fierce.

No matter what I'm doing, I'm always cognizant of how I'm talking to people and how I can say something differently in order to stand out.

But yeah, back to my childhood. No cable. No computers. No car phones (until my dad got one, but we sure as heck weren't allowed to use it—those minutes were expensive!). No camcorder or VCR. We did have a stereo that could connect to local radio stations and play records and tapes. We did get a CD player once they became mainstream and more affordable. We also had magazine subscriptions to publications like *Parents* and *Highlights* that my lovely grandparents paid for, as money was tight (divorce will do that). I was a curious kid, and I wanted information. That's why magazines were devoured. The nightly news, revered. And the barrage of questions aimed toward each parent remained constant.

During my new childhood in Atlanta, I remember how the kids who lived in neighborhoods, not so much my apartment complex, got to spend so much time together. And where were the parents? Gobs of kids all living in single-family homes on streets filled with other children that would spend hours playing outside together. I was in awe of this phenomenon, and I cherished every single invite when I got dropped off to join in the fun.

I did play outside for hours, running around, daydreaming, riding my bike, and roller skating solo around both my mom's apartment complex and my dad's condominium buildings. I had no other choice but to be creative as a kid. Whether solo or with my sister Jackie, babysitters, or friends—we played with Legos, organized colored pencils in a rainbow pattern, and built and imagined living in our Barbie houses.

This unstructured, pretend play allowed me to really explore and push through any perceived boredom. And creative free-play is so, so important even alone—but it didn't come with the same sense of fun (and safety in some cases) as did playing with my friends in their neighborhoods.

Many of those kids had televisions with fledging video game consoles. I recall going to a few friends' houses who had video game systems like Atari or Nintendo and me playing the motorcycle game or Super Mario Bros. for hours. I also remember how they had television sets with remote controls (*wait, you don't have to walk over to the TV to change a channel or adjust the volume?*), and that sure seemed incredibly luxurious. Do you remember the first time you hit the Mute button? The power we now wielded! Low-resolution, simple video games were a revolution for us. Yet somehow, we would grow tired of playing these 16-bit adventures and seek the comfort of playing outside. No one had to tell us to get off these devices. Ultimately, they were so basic we'd simply do it ourselves.

One of my very best friends in the entire world, Wade Beacham, a dad of two born in the late 70s, recalls,

> In the late 1980s into the early 90s I lived in a suburban neighborhood setting with children all up and down the street. While many kids were close in age to me, the majority of us went to different schools, public and private. We played inside and we played outside. Weekend days were majorly spent outside with Friday, and Saturday nights reserved for sleepovers and a lot of gaming.
>
> While we gamed for hours and hours into the night, I now feel a vast contrast to today's gaming setup and routine. The 80s and 90s gaming didn't isolate us in separate bedrooms or basements in separate houses; it collected us together in a single home, around a single gaming system. We would share by taking turns. With two controllers and five kids, the winner stayed, and the loser passed the controller. We had to cooperate to help each other get better. We had to beat the winner to unseat the prior games' victor. We had to occupy ourselves and each other with side games and conversation while waiting our turn.
>
> So much of the activity and the memories I hold to this day were inside that room but outside the video game. I can only wonder what, if any, of those good times and lessons learned are lost to a new generation of gamers. How dramatically different my experience is to a gamer in 2024, sitting alone in a dark room with a headset on.

Maybe all is not lost for siblings when it comes to gaming. In the early 90s I grew up with one sibling, a younger sister. We had very little in common and even attended different schools. I was often absent from the house as a multisport athlete, or just out with friends. The same scenario played out in my home as so many others. My younger sister would continually seek any sort of way to connect or gain my attention to spend any amount of time with her. One successful solution was that she found our mutual interest in adventure games on the gaming console.

She figured out how we could play a single-player/controller adventure "together." I would mostly play, and she would watch. By allowing me to play the game, she learned she had my captive audience and at least 10% of my attention that came with it. She would follow along as if my character or she would read the game map. She would help by reading about hints in the game to help inevitably figure out the correct path to advance the story. Sometimes, she would just sit there and sing aloud. Looking back, gaming with my sister may be some of the fondest memories I hold of her at that age.

—*W. Beacham, personal communication, 2024*

I love hearing stories like this. The 80s in particular was such a pivotal moment in time, when digital innovation was rapidly offering up new ways to connect and be entertained, yet we still had the solid grounding and traditions of generations past.

Early Media Impact on My Self-Esteem

My dad's place was much colder than my mom's apartment, in many aspects, but he did upgrade to cable eventually. We still weren't allowed to watch much TV (if any), and the few times that we could, it was nature shows, car racing, rock concerts, or preachers. We would frequently listen to all kinds of rock music on the radio or his vast record collection, which then turned into a tape collection, which then tuned into a CD collection, while we read books or played with our toys. We'd read the newspaper cover to cover, really anything we could get our hands on, including *Architectural Digest* and, oddly enough, *Women's Wear Daily* (a fashion-industry trade journal often referred to as the "Bible of Fashion").[2]

Like many men at the time, our Dad had a thing for looking sharp and keeping up with the hottest supermodels sporting the latest fashions. If I'm honest, none of this fashion culture of the 80s and 90s really helped my body image and self-esteem at the time, and there are traces of it negatively impacting me to this day.

Thankfully, I didn't have a constant feed that I carried everywhere with me to remind me that I wasn't tall and thin and dripping in designer threads and jewels. I looked at a magazine over the course of an hour, max; maybe flip through it twice if I was really bored; and then I was finished. I didn't put it in my pocket and pull it out and flip through it every five minutes. We had unattainable images of what women should look like all around us—in addition to magazines, there were billboards and television commercials and movie stars shown on the big screen. But we were not steadily inundated. We were also taught little sayings back then—for example, if we wanted ice cream, the phrase "One minute on the lips forever on the hips" would buzz in our subconscious. And if we wanted an extra pat of butter on our baked potatoes or another piece of pizza? Well, that's when "Nothing tastes as good as skinny feels" would creep up.

In those days, there were images featuring these airbrushed, scantily clad models not only throughout my father's condo in print but everywhere really. The culture at the time, overall, was much more okay with women (and some men) displayed as sex objects and incapable of doing much beyond that, despite the women's liberation movements from the not-too-distant 60s and 70s. Ironically, this was when many of these young mothers themselves were growing up.

When I was a little girl, I remember accompanying my mom to SYMS (an off-price retail clothing store chain that no longer exists) off Jimmy Carter Boulevard (a.k.a. the boonies if you live in Buckhead). We eventually made our way into the dressing room, which to my surprise was just a gigantic room with a lot of mirrors and a lot of women in various stages of dress…or undress.

I guess discount stores don't do doors? Maybe that's why they went out of business. Anyway, I looked around and noticed many things.

Granny panties
Weird bras

Cellulite

Saggy skin

Ill-fitting clothes

And of course, grown women with teeny, tiny, almost nonexistent boobs

This scared me.

I wanted so bad to be a woman and one with curves! To me, one of the pros that could make up for the "con" of a completely average body build with a thick, short torso and zero thigh gap was to have ample, soft, beautiful breasts.

From that moment on, I would fervently pray for boobs.

(And my period actually. Right?! I don't know why either.)

God sure has a sense of humor.

I went from a flat-chested 6th grade girl to a D-cup sporting woman who had periods every 28 days in two short years!

Talk about a game-changer. All of a sudden, I was pop-u-lar.

Boys who never gave me the time of day were suddenly interested in me, and not just for my Latin test answers. It was flattering and empowering, but for all the wrong reasons.

It was also incredibly distracting.

Some of my favorite memories are thinking about my first kiss in 7th grade—and I can't imagine if those fond reflections were replaced with fears and regrets surrounding pictures or videos I had sent before my brain was fully formed and able to make adult decisions. I'd be gutted.

Looking back, I wish I had held firm to my desire to learn everything I could academically, instead of shifting my intense focus to what people thought of me.

I went from being a straight A, honor roll, perfect-score-on-standardized-tests kind of student to a sometimes-making-Bs-and-Cs (the horror!) student.

I still got into the high school and college of my dreams (at the time), but I did not fully utilize the resources that were at my disposal.

I wish so desperately that I would have taken drama instead of worrying about who I was going to catch a ride with up to Blackburn Park so I could hang with the cool older kids who were smoking (all sorts of things).

I should have taken as many art classes as possible, instead of making an ass of myself as a basketball cheerleader. But participating in any kind of sport was the fastest way to obtain a letter jacket. The alternative—wearing a starchy navy blazer during the cold weather uniform portion of the year at my private Catholic high school—was both unflattering and not warm enough. I realize that with the right alterations most outfits can be made to look great on a human, but we could barely afford the private school tuition at a discount thanks to financial aid, much less a custom-tailored navy blue blazer.

I should have taken computer science and asked for help when physics and chemistry flew over my head, but I spent more time memorizing people's phone numbers and class schedules (so I could "accidentally" run into them, duh) than periodic tables and Newton's Law.

If I utilized the time I spent pouring over magazines figuring out how to lose weight and tone my "flabby" thighs to, I don't know, learn how to code instead, maybe I would have programmed something amazing and been able to afford a gym membership and a personal trainer instead of trying bulimia sophomore year of high school and the heart patient soup diet to drop 10 lbs in a week.

Is that not what a 14-year-old girl should be doing? Making sure she ingests no more than 1,200 calories per day, including lifesaver mints (because fresh breath is errrythang), which by the way are 15 calories each?

I'll never forget the feeling of buying a pair of size 2 forest green corduroys from The Gap and feeling like I had won at life. SO THIS IS WHAT IT FEELS LIKE TO BE SKINNY. So what if I'm starving. So what if I have only 70 calories left in my day so I'll have one piece of reduced calorie toast with "I Can't Believe It's Not Butter" spray for flavor. So what if my body and brain are still growing and I need to be nurtured emotionally, mentally, and physically? I'll just eat my feelings, throw them up, erode my esophagus, wear the enamel off my teeth, still hate my body, and cry myself to sleep.

I'm so glad my mom overheard me throwing up about a month into that phase and scheduled an appointment with a nutritionist at Piedmont Hospital. I don't remember her name, but I am so thankful for her taking the time to show me what a proper portion of food should look like and showing me what a healthy body should be. Newsflash: it wasn't the models on the cover of *Women's Wear Daily* back in 1995. #thighgap #heroinchic #cokediet.

Outside Influences Abound

Now, when you have divorced parents and they are dating long-term partners, the vibe changes. In our case, that's when it seemed the rules would flex a bit. My sister and I would be introduced more to outside cultural influences. They weren't all bad, of course. I'll never forget seeing Doritos and Pepsi in our kitchen for the first time ever (mom's boyfriend) or seeing lovely floral window valances one day in my dad's condo that were definitely not his style but added a touch of warmth, and Jackie and I were here for it. The prevalence of these new cultural and technological access points, be it the new Sega Genesis my mom's boyfriend kept at our apartment or the *Cosmopolitan* magazines my dad's girlfriend kept at his condo, seemed to grow.

I remember reading the book *Cheaper by the Dozen* when I was around 12 years old. I was the biggest book nerd (as reading was the one thing I was allowed to do with no time limits or rules; well, that and cleaning and praying). Why I remember reading it is significant. The story is about a family with a lot of kids and the dad's job is an efficiency expert. And I was like, "What? There are actually jobs that allow you, and pay you, to go in and tell companies how to be better? And how to do better?"

And after I read that, I think I said, "I want to do that. I have a lot of opinions. And of course, I think they're great. And I want to tell people how to do things better and how to stand out."

In a sense, that's what I get to do with this book as well. But not from a place of judgment without experience. It's absolutely from a place of *please don't make the mistakes that I and so many other parents made.*

Media Consumption Moves on Demand

The original on-demand viewing—owning a VCR—meant everyone could bring home the experience of the movie theater. Almost overnight, children and their parents would gather around the family television to watch a film together as a Friday or Saturday night ritual.

We would go to the nearby Blockbuster Video, or the small mom-and-pop video store on the corner, to wait at the counter for the newest releases to be returned. We'd order Domino's pizza (shout-out to thin crust pepperoni), have it delivered as if it was a novelty, and watch movie after movie. Sometimes with our parents in the room, but many times—if we could get away with it—without them.

The 80s were also a time where we saw the rise of slasher movies and horror films, which more often than not also featured young, buxom women falling victim to sexualized acts and violence. Figures like Jason from the *Friday the 13th* slasher series or Freddie Krueger from the *Nightmare on Elm Street* films grew popular, even celebrated, in our culture. These half-men, half-monsters were soon able to be taken home on VHS video as VCRs exploded in use during the second half of the decade.

It was also during this time that America, and the world, experienced the explosion of XXX videos, dirty movies, or pornography. It didn't take long for the exploitation of women in film via this genre to overtake this media. And the advent of cable television only propagated what was happening. More sex, more violence, cruder language, and more mature themes were appearing more frequently across all types of media. It was much like today but less amplified in terms of the places it's now available, and honestly—in terms of the level of unthinkable graphic and violent content that is portrayed alongside.

Sometimes Monsters Are IRL

Whether the monster was a fictionalized monster or not, my exposure to strangers, predators, sexual content, violence, scary news and world events, health misinformation, political unrest, drugs and alcohol, disordered eating, mental health issues, and suicide was still mostly contained to a few sources. Despite video killing the radio star, MTV music videos dominating the airwaves, and Blockbusters on every corner, exposure to adult topics was still somewhat limited. But children of today (and their friends) have one-click access to all of the above.

Not all dangers are digital, and here's part of my personal story to highlight that fact.

At one point, my own son was scared of the dark. I had been trying my best to convince him up, down, and sideways that there were *no* monsters, they absolutely were not real, and that he was totally safe inside the confines of our sleepy, suburban home. But, deep down inside, I knew that was a lie.

Because I had found a real-life monster through our church, of all places. He was awesome. So good with the kids. His dad was a preacher, I think, but not ours. And I literally begged my mom to let him babysit us. Keep in mind, I was a very convincing 6-year-old. My sister was 2. He was 17, maybe 18.

My monster was fun. He was polite. He had more energy than my other babysitters and let me call the shots. He let us run him ragged and was an excellent jungle gym. Eventually the fun had to end and we had to get to bed as per my mom's orders.

I needed help going to sleep at night. I shared a room with my baby sister, but still, I was a really anxious kid. It could have been the divorce or my genes, or Peter Gabriel's "Shock the Monkey" video I shouldn't have seen on MTV as a toddler or a combination of all three, but I did not like going to sleep at night in the dark without an adult in the room.

I had asked him to scratch my back, and he obliged. My mom was the best backscratcher where he was just so-so. Awkward. Clumsy. He started off as any normal back-scratching babysitter would but then did something different. And his hands were not on my back.

This is the point of the story that sucks.

This part is disturbing.

This part makes me part of a statistic.

And this is why I'm sharing it with you. We need to talk about childhood sexual abuse, especially in light of the fact that technology has exponentially increased the rate at which children are abused both in real life and online.

Mere seconds made me instantly aware of how my body felt when touched a certain way in certain places, way, way before an innocent little girl should have. Unfortunately, I would like to share more about what happened, those feelings, these feelings, and how it's continued to affect me but for the fear that there are still some people, creepy, hurt people, out there who get off on this stuff, so I won't expand here. Just know it happened repeatedly.

My experience with sexual abuse still breaks my loved ones' hearts. It's what my mom had tried to prepare me for with books about decrying "stranger danger" and the part my dad prayed would never happen to his little girls if he wasn't in the house to protect them.

This is the part of my story that I didn't even know was such a common story until two years later when I was watching cartoons on our green floral sofa and an NBC "The More You Know" special aired. This topic was meant to inform both children and their caregivers about the very real, and far too often, instances of childhood sexual abuse. As I sat there, I realized that I was the 1 in 4.

As with every childhood, there are parts that are still so crystal clear and yet other parts that remain cloudy, fuzzy, patchy, maybe even distorted.

The part that I don't remember most clearly is what happened when I told my mom that I believed I had been treated inappropriately and how we ended all contact with him.

Looking back, I know she was devastated. I can understand the full force of mommy guilt and how it envelops you with what can only be described right now as a nonverbal, beyond expressive "oof." This news? Oh, man. How do you deal? How did she deal? I can only imagine the impact of this knowledge on her when I think of how I might deal with something like this happening to my own.

I believe that, at age 8, I didn't want to confront him, talk to him, or certainly deal with any legal or judicial process that had to occur as a result of me speaking up. I wanted to simply move on. And my mom honored that. My fiercely strong, hard-working, single mom who loved me with every fiber of her being just wanted to make sure I was okay.

Somehow, I really think I was okay because she was with me through it all. She was on my side and provided everything that I felt I needed at the time. Understandably, at the time I was unable to really grasp the long-term or lasting effects that something like this produces. And I convinced her of that as well. Mom, I really hope you are not reading this because I don't want you to feel guilt or pain—not for one single second. It is *not* your fault. He fooled us all. But you were there when I needed you, and I'm stronger for it now.

Another cloudy account was my interaction with my dad at the time I told each parent. I can't recall his reaction. To this day, I don't like to talk about it with him because I know it hurts him so. But it did happen, and we can talk about it if he wants. Dad, I hope you are not reading this either.

A few years later, my monster suddenly appeared at the doorstep of my mother's apartment. We had certainly moved on. I have no idea as to the reason why he showed up, but he did. We hadn't pressed charges. We hadn't put him on blast on social media—that wasn't even a thing yet. We hadn't told his parents or his school or our church. We silently moved on.

I can only wager a guess as to why he was there. Maybe he was coming to apologize. Maybe he was coming to see if I remembered what happened and if I had told anyone. Maybe he was just still so sick. I don't know and my mother never told me what transpired at that doorstep. Perhaps this was her way to simply shield me from him because I remained hidden behind a door until he finally left.

Many, many years later—in January 2010—I took an innocuous, afternoon trip to the local birthday party supply store to pick out some colorful balloons for my beloved only son's first birthday party. That's where I saw my monster again. I looked up to see him behind one of the three registers at the front of the store. I had not thought about him in many, many years. I had not seen his face in my nightmares, couldn't recall his voice if you paid me. I had to center myself.

I really believed that my mind was just messing with me for a minute, but my body knew. My core knew. And as I reluctantly drew closer, like a slow-moving conveyor belt, every inch of my being knew.

He must have felt my stunned gaze, as he looked up. Our eyes met for a split second, and I couldn't hold the gaze. I instantly looked away, grasping to find something, anything on my smartphone where I could hide again—just like the door. I felt a sinking feeling as I simply mashed buttons and scrolled as feelings of falling riddled my adult body. Of course, once I got to the top of the queue his register became available. Without looking up from my phone, I spoke up and motioned for the lady behind me to go ahead. I don't remember what I said, but I'm sure I made something up. It was all cloudy again.

I remained lost in my smartphone and refused to look up to see if he even knew that I was actively avoiding him. Thankfully, another register opened, and I skirted over to it in a flash.

Before we exchanged any niceties, I suddenly blurted out to the half-asleep cashier, "Hey, is that [name]?

The cashier answered, "Yes, why? Do you want me to get him?"

"No!" I said emphatically, yet still, trying not to sound completely odd.

With that validation, the overwhelm only tightened its grip, as the daze completely engulfed me. It's not lost on me that the store I was leaving supported parties, crafted memories, and manifested celebrations *for children* and now here I was trying to put one foot in front of the other while also stuffing what seems like a quadrillion stubborn, helium party balloons into the back of my SUV and gathering my game face for my son's first birthday party. Funny how I can still remember that feeling. And those questions.

"How is this possible? Why did this happen? Oh, no! Oh my gosh, he works at a place that caters to kids. What if? What if my lack of action caused others to be hurt? Why didn't I speak up? Is he doing this to others right now? What if it was just me and he was a dumb teenager? What if it wasn't? What can I even do about it, 20-something years later?"

Well, after rallying to enjoy my only son's first birthday, I decided it was time to talk about what happened, to more than just my mom. I took to the Internet after I put my son to bed, wrote from my heart, posted the story to my blog, and shared it with a few close friends. I truly do not think this was a coincidence. This encounter happened for a reason. And by posting my story, it opened up doors (that's a theme you'll see here throughout my life) to connect authentically with moms across the globe and showcase my critical message of awareness and child safety to major media outlets. I'll talk about this more in a bit.

A few years later I saw my monster again (albeit online), ironically in the era of the #metoo movement. I Googled him after feeling empowered by my work at Bark Technologies escalating predators to law enforcement and saw that he had been repeatedly convicted of violent sexual abuse.

Technically, he was convicted in 2004 of "SEXUAL BATTERY (2ND OR SUBSEQUENT CONVICTION)—FELONY." As per Georgia Code 16-6-22.1, Sexual Battery is defined as intentionally mak-ing physical contact with the intimate parts of the body of another person without the consent of that person. The term "intimate parts" means the primary genital area, anus, groin, inner thighs, or buttocks of a male or female and the breasts of a female.

He was a known sex offender and had multiple mugshots posted online. And as of last look he was not behind bars, having either served his time or paid a really good lawyer. Those images of his face staring into the camera with his history deep behind his eyes will never leave my brain. His victims potentially could have been spared if I spoke up. It guts me to reflect on this, and I wish I could apologize to those survivors.

Admittedly, I still have never confronted him, but I did try to reach out to the authorities to report the incidents. Unfortunately, the statute of limi-tations for child sexual abuse that happened decades ago prevented any meaningful justice from happing. It was absolutely deflating.

I know I will continue to unpack this for the rest of my life. I do think everything happens for a reason, and I'm not angry with God or feel like He let me down. I know bad things happen to good people. And while I believe that I may have forgiven my monster, I certainly have not forgotten him. I lived a childhood where I was far more aware of my sexuality than I should have been and felt less than worthy in some instances as a result.

Why am I telling you this?

The more that people like me speak up, the less stigma that will be attached to this sort of abuse, and we can bring some of the darkest things that happen to kids into the light to unpack and prevent future instances.

Additionally, crimes that used to take place only in-person are now beginning, and sometimes remaining, entirely online. Thanks to the digital age, access and exposure to children is easier than ever for predators. According to the FBI, "There are more than 500,000 online predators active each day only and they all have multiple online profiles. More than 50% of victims are ages 12–15 and 89% of victims are contacted by online predators through chat rooms and instant messaging."[3]

On top of that, children now can instantly access information that isn't meant for their developing hearts, minds, and bodies. In many cases, the content and people children are exposed to online can make them more aware of graphic sexual content, violence, misinformation, comparison traps, and so many other complex adult issues that push good kids to make bad choices even sooner and faster than they otherwise would. This, right here, is the "why now" part of this chapter.

Believe it or not, this isn't a book about bashing tech. There is a positive, beneficial side of all this information sharing and connectivity as well.

The Intersection of Parenting and Tech

I'm a mom who has spent her entire career working in media—from traditional to digital to social. My focus has been the intersection of parenting and tech, with a specific mission to help keep kids safer online and in real life.

In fact, many years ago as a relatively new mom, I started a Facebook group called Parenting in a Tech World. Today, it has more than half a million parents as members. You might even be one of them. And any learnings that we can share with each other for how to do it better, I'll take that. I'll take all the help I can get, and this is an incredible group.

At the time, I was going to mom conferences and meeting brands, influencers, bloggers, and media outlets. I remember being awestruck and starstruck at first—meeting these vulnerable people in real life who shared very raw moments online with the world and offered (what I thought was) true connection in the form of storytelling. I also saw the darker side of it. It was big business. So many of these momfluencers, family bloggers, and YouTubers had so many self-centered, narcissistic parts to themselves, and some were full on exploiting their children.

But the biggest reality was how these moms didn't have it all figured out. No parent has ever had to parent in a world like this. And while I came to the understanding that maybe they didn't know what they were really saying or promoting, they did have solid Instagram feeds and followings they were beginning to monetize. These people had insecurities just like me and also depended on audiences for revenues.

This idea of the self-appointed (lifestyle, fitness, parenting, you name it) expert happens a lot still. Especially in the wake of the coronavirus pandemic, the reemergence of podcasting, the explosion of ChatGPT, and the constant drip of pro- and anti- everything in our society.

As I watched this user-generated content (UGC) lifestyle expert movement emerge and given my background in media and marketing, I dabbled in blogging but never really felt comfortable sharing photos of my son online. I eventually deleted 99.9% of his digital footprint from the Internet, the remaining 0.01% being things I can't find/can't remember existing or he's given me explicit permission to share or he's shared himself on his (hopefully) private accounts. I'm so thankful I didn't jump headfirst into the world of putting my son on display for the world to watch like *The Truman Show*, all while supporting our "lifestyle" with sponsored content. For a brief moment it made sense, and empowered moms and dads generated income while giving them the ability to stay at home. The long-term consequences though of putting child content online are still emerging, and my heart goes out to those children who did not consent or have no savings to show for it. My heart also goes out to the parents who now know better and do better and regret sharing so much of their children online.

To recap, right now, I'm the chief parent officer and chief marketing officer of Bark Technologies. We are a tech company that helps to keep kids safer online and in real life with an app that helps parents monitor and manage their children's digital world, an in-home physical device that helps to monitor and limit screen time on things like gaming consoles and smart TVs, free software for schools across the United States (our giveback) that has escalated credible school shooting threats and predators to law enforcement, a safer smartphone for kids that I wish existed when my son was younger, and a smartwatch for those children who aren't yet ready for a safer smartphone.

Our mission is to keep kids safer online and in real life, and for my team, it's all-encompassing.

And because of my career in this space, because of Bark's massive, far-reaching footprint, I can influence and help people in a way that's far beyond my wildest dreams. I like to think that despite only having one biological child, I am still able to be a mother to now more than seven million children across the nation. Our work is heavy, but the fact that we are saving children's lives daily keeps us steadily moving forward.

Why Now

So much has changed, and quickly. We're all still figuring out what it means for children and modern childhood (both good and bad) and what we could do about it to mitigate the harms and enhance the benefits.

No other parent in the history of parenting on this planet has had to do what we're doing. And we can't turn to our parents and ask for advice in the same way they could ask their parents for typical childhood developmental milestones. I can't call my mom and ask her for advice on when I should let my child have Snapchat or how I should navigate conversations with him about online pornography because she didn't have to deal with this, nor did my grandmother.

What I can do, however, is ask my network on LinkedIn who I should talk to about growing up online. And boy did my network come through with an introduction to Dr. Carl Marci, physician, scientist, entrepreneur, and author. He's a board-certified psychiatrist and has been seeing patients through Mass General Hospital in Boston for more than 20 years. He says it's an incredible field, and part of what attracted him to it is that there weren't two psychiatrists who truly practiced the same way.

In his 2022 book *Rewired: Protecting Your Brain in the Digital Age*, Dr. Marci uses a metaphor about the 1908 Model T—the horseless carriage. Remember the famous quote from Henry Ford that reads "If I asked the people what they wanted, they'd have said a faster horse"?

Well, the car was the revolutionary new technology that was all the rage around the turn of the century. But through his innovation in mass production and the simple law of increasing supply, the early car immediately became more accessible for the masses. See, prior to the Model T, the cost equivalent in today's dollars would be more than \$100,000. In short, very few people had cars.

But Ford's Model T changed all that. Almost overnight, the car was affordable for tons and tons more people. So, there was this massive influx of cars—cars everywhere with no rules of the road. Children died. Adults died. Farm animals died. It was pure chaos. It took 10 years before there were any rules set.

In fact, 10 years went by before the first stop sign was introduced and made. It was another three years before the patent for the stoplight was filed. America went on a 100-year journey of making roads safer with better signage, better lights, airbags, sensors, power brakes, seat belts, and so on.

The crazy thing is that vehicle death numbers went down and down continuously year after year until 2016 when they started to tick back up.

Can you guess why?

Because people now had smartphones in their cars. In other words, people were distracted.

What technology has brought us has been transformative. And it's also been too much, too fast, and too soon. A massive positive is, ironically, how screens have also helped us connect with loved ones in real time in other time zones and even heal with telehealth opportunities. Think about the boom of Zoom over the COVID-19 pandemic. Sure, the majority of its growth came from business simply trying to stay afloat, but why did we need to see each other? Friends and groups of people and families set up Zoom calls to see and hear from the people they cared about.

Zoom was a vital lifeline for so many people. Formally, educators and helping professionals like physicians and psychologists changed their entire practices so they could do it over a video conference. This technology helped the helpers help us during that time and through today. It helped us all heal from it, heal from each other, heal overall. But there's a good reason why we could benefit from seeing and hearing a caregiver over perhaps just hearing their voice on a voice call.

I also think about my own unique journey. I'm one of the few who had an analog childhood, then a digital transition in high school, college, and my young twenties. My career started in traditional media, and while I was in the traditional media space, it quickly became digital, Internet, social media. I know that social media exacerbates the innate need to fit in, jump on bandwagons, and copy the influencers. And so I lived it in real time, but thankfully through an adult lens.

As the information economy has exploded, we (adults, society, legislators, healthcare professionals, educators) have neglected to prioritize the physical, mental, and—if it's important to you—spiritual well-being of our most vulnerable population: children who were born any time after the year 2000.

I've had the opportunity to be on a lot of big stages, whether it's talking to Fox News, NBC, CBS, ABC, you name it, I've been there. And most people would think that would be slightly terrifying, and during some of those instances, it very well was. But nothing to date has been scarier than trying to raise my son in this over-connected, under-protected age.

So in summary, I've been through the wringer personally, I've spent more time analyzing the state of childhood today as it pertains to the rapid digital transformation over the past few decades than most, and I've dedicated my life to helping others, especially children.

While I'm not a doctor or a neuroscientist, people keep asking me to share what I know and what they can do to help their kids—and so I will do that for you here, now, and over the next few chapters.

Occasionally, I'll reflect back on my life to date—both personally and professionally—to add color to the contrast of how we got here and why we need to do something about it.

Ultimately, the contents within this book can help you make the best decisions you can with the information we have at this time. That's all any of us can really do—control what we can and lean on others to help us along the way.

Thank you again for joining me. Let's do this together.

Notes

1. Bowman, R. (2005). Prescription for crime. *TIME*. https://time.com/archive/6671700/prescription-for-crime/.
2. Wikipedia (2024). *Women's Wear Daily*. https://en.wikipedia.org/wiki/Women's_Wear_Daily.
3. KOAA News5 (2021). Deep dive: FBI estimates 500,000 online predators are a daily threat to kids going online. https://www.koaa.com/news/deep-dive/fbi-estimates-500-000-online-predators-are-a-daily-threat-to-kids-going-online.

2 | The Good Old Days

There's a reason why (regardless of the specific decade our loved ones are referring to) the past is so often called "the good old days." Times were simpler, perhaps, and hindsight is always 20/20. In the process of writing *Parenting in a Tech World* (in 2020) and working with the directors and producers of *Childhood 2.0* that same year, the past became an even more staggering benchmark for documenting just how much has changed for children just over the course of the past century.

For example, my grandmother, born in 1922, spent her childhood helping her mother care for her three brothers after her father's untimely passing during the Great Depression. She knew how to make her own clothes and utilized an icebox, not a refrigerator, to keep food cold in their home. Fast forward to today, where children can order both clothes and food to be delivered to their homes within an hour via a smartphone.

In this chapter, we will compare past and present methods for seeking knowledge and accomplishing tasks, and we will set the stage for the discussion of generational differences in the role of technology. Because the past is such a powerful teacher, we must revisit and reflect before holistically moving forward.

This chapter also discusses the difficulties faced by parents operating in a digital world who grew up in a much more analogical world. By the time you've finished reading this book you will better understand how modern childhood differs from the upbringing most parents experienced.

You will have more clarity around some of the things that might have been frustrating you, and you will learn some tools and techniques to make the adjustments needed today for effective parenting.

Historical Context

As a society, we've moved from gathering around a fire, storytelling, and writing on walls to getting our information and connecting with others seemingly out of thin air (radio, television, the Internet) pretty rapidly.

To see how we landed on to the current state of smartphones and global connectivity, it might help to review some general technological and societal advancements of the past 40 years.

Going from zero to Google over the last four decades that I've been on this planet means firsthand exposure to unprecedented and rapid societal change.

In 1980, I was birthed onto a complex rock flying around the sun in the Milky Way universe where it wasn't unusual to see:

- People smoking indoors and on airplanes! (In fact, according to the authors of "The changing public image of smoking in the United States: 1964–2014," "…smoking was permitted nearly everywhere: smokers could light up at work, in hospitals, in school buildings, in bars, in restaurants, and even on buses, trains and planes."[1])
- Parents, teachers, babysitters, and childcare providers physically disciplining children (anyone out there still remember the sheer terror of knowing you had a spanking coming?).
- Families hurrying home to catch the nightly news or a specific show at a specific and limited time because there was no DVR or highlight of clips to watch on YouTube, Instagram, or TikTok after the fact.
- Children riding bikes without helmets.
- Young children riding in cars without car seats and older children and adults without seatbelts.
- The local mall packed with teenagers, and not just around the holidays.
- Phones that had to be connected to a landline, outlet, or wall in order to work and that utilized a rotary dial function or keypad.

- People walking around *without* giant, expensive metal insulated beverage holders in their hands. (As of time of writing, Stanley cups are the craze. Before that, Yeti was all the rage. I'm eager to see who emerges as the new liquid leader in the consumer space.)
- Car windows that had to be manually cranked up or down—not just by pushing a button.
- Children in restaurants, churches, and other spaces that required them to sit still and be quiet (or at least respectful) without an electronic babysitter.
- People talking to each other as they stood in line, anywhere, instead of face down on a phone.
- Commercials and infomercials that were clearly delineated and limited to either a 2-minute interruption in-between your favorite shows, or sometimes, a full 30-minute block in the wee hours of the morning. Either way, you knew that someone was trying to sell something. It was clear. Now—the lines are blurred.

Impact of Technology

Believe it or not, before everyone had a phone in their pocket, notifications came in the form of:

- A ringing phone from a room where the phone was plugged into a landline. (If you had means, chances are you had multiple phones in multiple rooms with multiple phone lines.)
- A flag up on a mailbox or mail in your mailbox. Sometimes, a loved one who sent you something would spill the beans to inform you to expect something in the mail, which would send you outside to check the mail multiple times a day. That's the old-school version of swiping to refresh your email inbox on your phone today.
- Knock on the door/doorbell ring. This sound was definitely an alert that you had visitors at your home. Delivery drivers. Your children's friends. Your friends. Showing up unexpectedly wasn't seen as rude or *sus* (see Chapter 11 for what *sus* means); it was just what we did.
- A barking dog. This generally preceded the knock or ring to let you know there was a potential danger. (Also, does this help you understand why Bark Technologies is named as such?)

- Sirens. Weather sirens, which are still in use, were largely depended upon in the event of bad weather. Police and emergency medical vehicles sounding their sirens helped you to know to be careful and get out of the way, versus today where those sounds "encourage" youth and adults alike to start live-streaming instead of steering clear or helping.
- The test of the emergency broadcast system. Usually, a tone would announce the test of an emergency by local officials. But ultimately, we'd always simply just hear the test itself.
- Road signs or the authorities setting up a roadblock to alert us of a situation ahead.
- Milk cartons and posters on telephone poles would let us know of missing children.

Generational Perspectives

When it comes to parents seeking information, we also turn to each other. We turn to those people who share similar experiences. Of course, that Google search comes in handy, but now with social media it also makes sense to crowdsource like-minded people. As of writing this book, the most popular places for that conversation to take place with parents are Facebook Groups, Instagram comments, text threads, and Reddit.

Just to underline this point, I did a little experiment to find answers to some big questions around this very subject. I wanted to find out what other caregivers believed regarding how the childhood experience is different today from when that parent was growing up. And just to be super meta (yes, pun intended), I decided to use Meta's flagship product, Facebook, to record their answers. So here's the question I posed to my Facebook Group of fellow parents[2]:

> Beyond technology (if it's even possible to separate that), how do you think your child's upbringing differs from your own in terms of values, expectations, freedoms, play, routines, social interactions, and/or day-to-day life?

I've already listed many of the answers I received in the list earlier in the chapter. For some, they've heard about this not-too-distant past before. For others, it could be somewhat news. But I think that this demonstrates, in a fairly simple way, the power of purely asking questions.

The sheer fact that I, as one single human, could in a matter of moments go to a place and ask a question that had the potential to be seen by at least 541,800 other humans (that's the group size at the time of writing—by the time you read this it very well might have doubled) for "free" is remarkable.

Free is in quotes because social media has a cost, but we will get to that in a little bit later in this book.

Within an hour of posting, there were 74 thoughtful comments from other parents, and the post had been seen by 2,000 people. Within 1 day of posting, 231 people had commented, and 11,500 eyeballs had seen the content therein.

Regardless, I wanted to get a sense of what a fully nonconnected life was like directly from the people who lived it. This would be the people who some might call the Baby Boomers. (And if you really want to be cool and hip, roll your eyes anytime someone their age says something and say "Okay, Boomer.") Ironically, it's a similar minimalizing trope, akin to the adage "Never trust anyone over 30," famously declared by those who were once under 30.

The Boomers are the generation that came just before me—they are my parents. They followed the Greatest Generation—you know, the people who won World War II and saved America? Somehow, they also precede Generation X—which is this sandwich generation which I don't really know if I'm a part of or not (the cutoff year is the year I was born), but I do know they are really, really into brooding and being fiercely independent.

Personal Reflections and Insights

I sat down to get some interviews from parents and grandparents of generations past, and I can't thank these lovely humans enough for going back in time, on the record, for all of us.

Barbara, a grandmother and the youngest of four siblings with married parents; Pittsburg, Pennsylvania

> Growing up in the 1950–60s I would wake up with excitement, hurriedly eat my breakfast, and dash out of the house to go play, whether it be on foot, my skateboard or my bike. My mom had no fear of my whereabouts, and I was free to go as I pleased, as long as I came back for lunch, or if I was playing in the afternoon, I had to be home by 6 p.m. for dinner. As the dinner hour approached, if I was close by, I would hear my mom as she stood on the porch calling for me and my sister!

As children we felt safe and were free to play in the woods, ride our bikes to the candy store, play hide and seek at night, and so much more. Most people kept their doors unlocked. There were no computers or cell phones. We spent our childhood for the most part outdoors, and if we were indoors, we were reading or using our imagination for make-believe play. I had a child-sized upholstered chair that also rocked. I remember turning it upside down and putting it on the living room floor that was carpeted in blue. In my imagination the blue carpet was the ocean, and the chair was my boat. I would spend hours "sailing and fishing."

We did not have electronic devices like the youth of today, we used our minds to create, and we were much more physically active. And our communication with our friends was in person. Occasionally, we would talk with them on the phone, but that would be brief. We were so lucky and blessed to have a childhood free from the fears of being kidnapped or harmed, the ability to play without our parents having to look out the window to keep us in view for fear of a predator. It was truly the most magical of childhoods, an era forever cherished.

Growing up in the 50s through the 70s we did not encounter the issues that the youth of today face. Because there were no cell phones or electronic devices, we didn't have to deal with sexting, shaming, online predators, or FOMO. Bullying was rare. There was not the epidemic of tweens and teens wanting to take their own life; in fact, I don't remember that ever happening. There were drugs, such as pot, LSD, hashish, and alcohol, but no one was lacing them with fentanyl. You didn't hear of people dying from them.

Occasionally you would hear of some teenagers who were drinking and speeding or racing. I do remember two high school guys dying after doing so. What seems so odd now is that my high school had an outside smoking area, and of course more than just cigarettes were smoked there. Our gym classes were not coed, and we had to wear gym uniforms. Of course other than the tacky uniforms, the worst part of that was being picked last for a team. Through grade school and into junior high (7–9 grades) girls were not permitted to wear pants. If it was a very cold or snowy day, the girls could wear snow pants under their skirt or dress, but once they got to school, they had to take the pants off.

At some point in junior high I started a petition to enable girls to wear pants, and it worked! We were finally free to wear pants! Since the junior high and high school weren't very close to my house, my mom would take us to school, but typically we would walk home, which was about 3 miles.

If we ran into a problem, we would have to find a payphone to call home or ask to use a phone in a shop. I don't remember there being school buses. And most families had only one car. Most moms stayed home and took care of the home and children. Fathers would be dropped off to take a bus or streetcar to work. There was typically one landline in the home. There was no call waiting or answering machines.

As a teenager, my girlfriends and I would often hitchhike, and we never ran into a leery situation. I can't imagine a teenager doing that today. There was no Uber; we had taxi cabs, but we rarely used them. We got around mostly by walking. There were cliques in school. The cheerleaders/ football players and those who were rich were called "cakes."

Then, there were the hippies/flower children, as well as the nerds and band people. Some of us interacted across the groups. Ritalin and Adderall was not around then. If you had trouble keeping up with assignments, you were pretty much on your own. Parents didn't help with homework.

Children were taught right from wrong and respected their elders and people's property. But the exception to that was the night before Halloween, called Devil's Night. If you were deemed a mean neighbor, you would probably get your house egged or trees TP'd. On Halloween we were free to go out trick or treating on our own and we were handed full-sized candy bars! Minis didn't exist back then. Of course, we were also given home-baked treats, without fear of being tainted.

—Personal communication, 2024

I don't know about you, but when I read Barbara's reflections, I am taken back to a time before I existed but longed for, for the most part. Her words convey what I imagine a quintessential childhood to be: freedom, exploration, resilience. We've obviously made strides in terms of public health awareness (no longer allowing children to smoke cigarettes on campus) and equal rights for women (no pants allowed?! What?!)—but on the flipside, her story conveys a sense of safety to me that this current generation and their parents do not share. Kids today are riddled with anxiety, while their parents are tracking their location in real time.

Linda, a grandmother of three and a parent of one; Springfield, Illinois

I see a big difference in the experience of childhood now compared to when I was a kid! The most noticeable is the lack of playtime that I see in today's kids. I remember being outside, even in Illinois, most of the time playing with all the neighborhood kids.

All age groups played together. We broke into groups, and many times the groups varied from day to day. We played on dirt hills and in puddles, played organized baseball and football, climbed trees…all without much adult supervision! We had wars with other groups, picked on younger kids and got picked on by the older kids. No adult interference unless someone got hurt!

We had to entertain ourselves most of the time and didn't have computers and tablets for entertainment or to be our babysitters. We mainly watched an hour or so of TV with our parents at night, and it was largely a communal experience. Totally family entertainment, and you wouldn't dare imagine hearing profanity or backtalk by the kids in those families.

Television was a big thing, though. And the only time we watched TV on our own was Saturday mornings when most programming were either cartoons or shows like the *Lone Ranger, Sky King*, or *Roy Rogers*. In all of these shows, we always had the good guys always doing the right thing and beating the bad guys. We would play the characters in these shows. I would play Roy Rogers, and my cousin Donna was Gale Evans, his wife. We did a lot of pretending. That is one thing I don't think that today's kids know how to do, pretend! Pretending prepares us for life experiences!

We also played a lot of games and made up our own games! Even as teenagers, we played card games with our mom and her best friends. We rode our bikes everywhere. We would ride for miles and miles back and forth to the little neighborhood store to buy stuff for our mom and buy some penny candy with the leftover change! We had no fear, and our parents didn't either. We felt safe, and our parents didn't worry about us if we were outside playing all day. There just wasn't the horror stories that you hear today about kidnappings and people hurting kids on purpose.

Sure, we still had bullies, but everyone knew who they were, and they usually pushed you around and did not fight with words behind the "safety" of a cell phone or social media.

I remember our neighborhood bully was really obnoxious, though. He would always pick on little kids. One time he went too far and was taking stuff away from the little kids and making them cry. I was a year older but a girl! I warned him that if he hit them again, I would go after him. Well, he did and so I did! I was in fifth grade, and he was in fourth grade, and I beat the stew out of him. People asked him at school how he got the black eye, and he would tell! But that was it, we handled things ourselves. There were never any parents to get involved unless things were really bad. We handled things ourselves, and that's a trait I think we used from playing and pretending and watching the good guys win.

—Personal communication, 2024

Free play. Pretend play. Communal play. Screens in the common areas of the home and limited screen time. A shared sense of responsibility and decency surrounding content standards if children were to be the intended audience. Much of what shaped Linda's childhood is now being used as novel suggestions to help struggling families. Ironic, huh?

Robert, parent of 6 and grandparent of 20; Los Angeles, California

I keep gravitating to the word *respect* when it comes to the primary differences between how I was raised and how children today are raised. When I say respect, I mean respect for the law. Police officers and law enforcement seemed like an honorable profession. Not only kids, but many adults had admiration for the men and women who did those jobs.

I guess it came from the fact that all of our parents were in World War II. They all pulled together, they all pulled for each other to literally save the world so Americans were much more united in that regard. There are so many videos today where interactions with police officers are so ugly. And yes, I'm aware that it goes both ways, but it's hard to imagine cussing out a police officer to me and there not being any repercussions.

Which means manners were something much more stressed. I can't imagine speaking to my father the way that many of these kids today speak to their parents. It was always "yes, sir," "no, sir," "yes ma'am," "no ma'am." We would call our parents friends Mr. or Mrs., never by their first names. In fact, any adult would be spoken to with extreme obedience, and we'd listen to them, too.

I've found that a lot of parents these days want to treat their kids as equals or, worse, friends. I don't understand that thinking. It's almost like they don't want their kids to get mad at them. Like I would tell my guys, I'm your parent, I'm not your friend, and I don't want to be your friend.

Technology was pretty basic stuff. We only had three channels on our black and white TV. We had family dinner together, and everyone had to be quiet so my dad could watch the news on the TV. And that's primarily where we got all our news of the world. My dad would talk back to the anchor like the anchor was somehow listening. Only when it was something that he didn't disagree with and when he'd really talk back or shout at the television or the presenter.

In a sense, it seemed like people were more aligned when I was a kid. It was the 50s and the GIs were back from the war. We did not have computers for information. We had to read books and encyclopedias for information. We had to go to school and hear what our teachers would have to say to us. We would all listen to the presidents when they'd address the nation. It didn't seem as contentious then...until the 60s, of course.

Safety wasn't really a thing. We never used seat belts or helmets on our bikes. I remember adults bringing alcoholic beverages along for the ride. We knew but we didn't have the scientific or political influence that made safety so vital as it is now. Maybe because our parents gave us more independence. **Collectively, they thought kids would simply figure things out themselves.** We created our fun or used our imagination because the adults weren't really around to oversee us. Sure, we could get into some trouble or misdeeds but they were fairly benign. In other words, no big deal. We didn't destroy property or steal. I'm sure there was some of that, but it was really few and far between. Anything like that would be handled by the authorities by contacting the parents. And they'd definitely handle it, some more sternly than others.

> I'd say today it seems like parents, especially men, are much more involved in their kids' lives. Parents today do more and actively are a part of entertaining their kids. But we could ride our bikes and walk to the park to play ball with our friends freely all over town. Everyone would look out for everyone else's kids. We didn't have to worry about child predators as much; there was the proverbial boogeyman, but they weren't really as known nor covered in the media like it is today. I'm sure they were out there, but it wasn't as known.
>
> I'd say today, everybody is so busy. There's just so many more people now with so many different cultures or walks of life. Everyone now kinda does what they do and keeps more to themselves. It's just different. In some ways better, in some ways worse. Just different.
>
> —*Personal communication, 2024*

Robert casually highlights two key trends that factor strongly into the contrast between the good old days and today, and I'll cover those more a bit later in this book. First, he touches on the concept of parents wanting to be their child's friend instead of their parent—and how that might be doing more harm than good. We see that represented in a variety of ways, including the decline in respect for authority. Second, he mentions kids figuring things out on their own, as they grow. The lack of parental hovering and swooping in to problem solve every little tiff helped previous generations build a level of resilience we do not see reflecting in today's youth.

Jean-Jacques, parent of three and grandfather of three, school principal/administrator

> Clearly, there is a massive focus on screens, much more so today than when I was growing up on TV. Far too much screen time. I have three children, and our approach is to customize the allocation to age and need, and demonstrate personal responsibility. The older children have more freedom while the younger have more oversight and regulation. Seeing the violence or sexualized content in games can't be good for young minds. While the research doesn't support a negative influence per se, I'd think anything you practice repeatedly will show up in your habits and interactions, and not all children are savvy at navigating appropriate interactions.

There are 21st century needs, preferences, and earned privilege that influence the time, access, and tools we allow our children to have. I mean, when I had my first phone, a 2003 classic Nokia, multiple digit clicks for simple texting was $0.25 per text sent. Hysterical. Needless to say, cell phones have changed just a bit.

As an educator, I do see value in today's tools but the explosion of tools and their integration into the academic experience has been scatterplot. Some school systems have minimum requirements for students on certain platforms and those platforms have algorithms that demonstrate how they positively impact student achievement, but it's really a time on task benefit; the more you do something, naturally, the better you get, so I'm not sold on that methodology.

Students do not understand the impact their actions can have. They take what could be a typical "playground" nonissue of teasing that can get amplified because there is a digital footprint and evidence. Just about every child has made jokes of "I'm going to beat you up" or "I could kill you" or some other innocuous threat. But that gets lost in translation via a digital tool, and then we have a major crisis, fear, bullying or some other hurtful consequence. Children lose the ability to navigate those soft and hard social skills and clearly are not ready for a digital record of their growing experience. Looking back, I know I'm very glad that social media wasn't around while I was growing up. I know we did some very foolish things, but they were *not* documented, mind you. Not one bit.

No one really knows where we go moving forward. But despite the backlash we sometimes see, I don't see any significant reduction. We'll definitely see more, both an increase in access and the ubiquitous presence of personal devices at even younger ages. Technology is getting integrated into eye glasses and clothing, so it will be everywhere, all the time. I hope we can just be smart about it.

—Personal communication, 2024

Jean-Jaques states something that I have heard repeatedly across a wide swath of adults over the age of 30: "I'm so glad I didn't have social media growing up." If so many humans whose frontal lobes are fully formed share the same sentiment, it's time we start paying attention.

Irmela, mother of two and grandmother of five

When I think about my upbringing, I have the fondest memories of my parents and my siblings. I was born during World War II as the sixth child. Our family lived in Berlin and was evacuated after the war to a small town in the northern part of Germany. Soon after that we settled in Wetzlar, a smaller town where my father worked as a civil engineer at a company called Buderus.

He rented a house that looked like a castle and had room for our very large family. We had another little sister after me; we were six girls and one brother. My mother was a homemaker and the most loving person in the world.

Growing up with a lot of siblings helped our self-esteem. There was always somebody close by when we ran into trouble. We always had playmates when we could not find anybody on our children-rich street. Across from our house was a huge mansion with an enormous park behind it, which stood almost empty all the time and belonged to the occupational forces after the war.

That park was our playground, and our parents always knew where we were and could call out for us if they wanted us home. We were raised strict but with lots of love. We could walk to school with our friends and siblings and played outside as soon as we were done with homework. We had to be home for lunch and dinner at a set time because it was mandatory to have the meals as a family all together. We enjoyed talking with our parents and each other and had friends over multiple times since there was always fun in a big group like that.

Since my parents had to monitor so many children, my father founded a Golf and Tennis Club with other members from his company where we could also spend our afternoons and weekends with friends in a gated facility with little worries for our parents.

We had no phones except the house phone on my father's table which we were allowed to use when we wanted to talk to our friends. There were no computers to keep in touch with friends, meaning our parents had a pretty good eye on us most of the time.

Thinking back to the time when our children grew up, we wanted to keep such a healthy and loving relationship with them. There were rules and restrictions but with a wider range of responsibilities. They could skip German school for an important soccer game or swim practice for a spend-the-night-party. They did not have their own phones and computers came into the picture when they went off to college. I often think how I would have handled the advantages of the Internet when they grew up. It sure is an advantage for them and their future to grow up in a world of science and technology at their fingertips.

—*Personal communication, 2024*

Irmela's story highlights a unique advantage that families of means have—the ability to problem-solve using material resources and tight-knit communities. So many children do not live in a dual-parent household or places that are safe and informed enough to collectively protect their children. Again—the good old days theme shines through.

Eike, father of two and grandfather of five

I was born as the youngest of four children (one girl, three boys) just a few weeks after WW II ended. My mother had just completed an incredible escape journey from East Prussia via Berlin to a small village near Hannover, highly pregnant with me and with three children ages 3, 5 and 8.

The little backpacks and some hand-carried bags contained everything the little family owned at that time, and my dad, an officer in the German Army, was unaccounted for. It was unknown if he was captured by British, Russian, French, or American forces or if he even was still alive. Luckily, the family reunited and was able to rebuild a normal life. My childhood was exciting and fun; we were happy with what we had and appreciated little things. My first "Lederhosen" were worn by my two brothers before they were handed down to me; so were most of the clothes I wore and the toys I played with. I got my first bicycle when my oldest brother got a new one, my middle brother inherited his bike, and I ended up with the leftover.'

The schools we attended were in four different locations all over town, and we would take public transportation, ride a bike, or occasionally walk. Nobody was taken or picked up by car – for the longest time we didn't even have a car.

Discipline was an absolute key in our childhood. Because our father was frequently on the road, my mother had to raise us mostly without him. We had to obey strict rules in our everyday life. If any of us was not on time for family meals, they would not get any food until the next regular meal. There were no extras; what was served was to be eaten. No arguments.

We had a simple radio for getting the latest news as well as some entertainment. I remember listening as a teenager to the Saturday afternoon "Country Music Hit parade" on American Forces Radio (AFN) and dreaming about one day traveling to the United States of America. The family bought their first TV when I was 17 years old, and we only could watch what our parents selected (there were only two TV stations available).

Communication with friends and relatives in other parts of the country was limited primarily to writing letters. Telephones were sparse and expensive; postage was a nickel. When I moved a hundred miles away from the town where my girlfriend lived, we started to exchange hundreds of letters to stay close to each other. We saved money for the occasional long distance phone call and train ride to meet in the middle and managed to maintain our close relationship for 63 years and still going strong (married for 52 years).

Our parents were born into turbulent times suffering from two world wars and unimaginable hardships. Children had to fit in and basically obey orders and instructions. That started to change with my generation: individual freedom of mind, anti-authoritarian thinking, and cross-border friendships have created the longest peaceful period in history.

Our children experienced technological advancement at incredible speeds that we hardly were able to follow. And our grandchildren are in the middle of another technological explosion that their parents have to master in order to stay connected with them.

—*Personal communication, 2024*

Eike's reflections remind me of a controversial (yet true) quote by G. Michael Hopf, author of *Those Who Remain*, that continues to hold firm to this day: "Hard times create strong men. Strong men create good times. Good times create weak men. And, weak men create hard times." Part of the impetus of this book is the hope that by becoming more aware of our lack of parental control, we can reverse the impeding future of weak men (and women) and hard times.

James, father of a 15-year-old

> The biggest difference between my childhood and my son's is the physical environment. And to be honest the physical environment for my son is much safer than mine was.
>
> For example, when I was 15, I would get home from school and spend the entire rest of the day playing in the woods with my friends. We had our own little world where we built forts, played games, explored, and talked about life.
>
> We also later used this freedom to experiment with alcohol, cigarettes, and even drugs. We were able to do all this experimenting because we were hidden in the woods from our parents.
>
> They had no idea what we were doing but were certainly aware of and okay with us being in there for hours and hours unsupervised. And it is exactly during that time when we did things we were not supposed to do as 15-year-olds. For a lot of people my age who grew up during those times, this was the time when we had our first sip or first puff that later led so many to a life of alcoholism or addiction to cigarettes or, even worse, an addiction to drugs.
>
> But today my son, as a 15-year-old, comes home from school and goes straight to his room to hang out with his friends virtually. They play games, explore, build forts virtually together, and talk about life just like we did.
>
> Only he is doing it in the safety of his own room, in our house, under our roof. And at least for now, he is not taking his first sips or his first puffs like I was at his age because the current environment that he interacts with his friends is completely different and not at all hidden from his parents.
>
> —*Personal communication, 2024*

James's account gives me more pause than the rest, because it immediately highlights three scary trends. First, children are more "sheltered" (inside the majority of the time) yet isolated than ever. Second, screens are rapidly replacing in-real-life human interaction, which our children so desperately need. And finally, predators. Given that there are more than 500,000 predators online at any given time according to the FBI,[3] I would venture to say that a large percentage of children have interacted with a seemingly nice "friend" online that was trying to befriend and groom them. I sincerely hope that is not the case for James's son, and I also hope that James has had multiple, candid conversations with him about this type of risk. I'll be sharing more conversations to have with your children a bit later in this book.

***

Most of those accounts are two generations from the kids growing up right now. Your kids. These are the grandparents of today who are witnessing the changes that we see in childhood.

Since I was the next generation, we carried the legacy of our Boomer parents, yet knew the world was changing. In all these accounts, I am struck by the amount of freedom and joy these grandparents had without, in some cases, any television sets at all. There is a very real fondness for a time where technology seemed to not be so pervasive, so oppressive, really.

I grew up where the elementary school or the library was the place to find information until the Internet became a thing. In fact, my very first "computer class" consisted of us learning how to type without looking at a keyboard and playing Oregon Trail. That was just a 16-bit, green and black screen that captivated all of us. I'm still freaked out by Typhoid and Dysentery to this day if you know what I mean.

I had to type out school assignments (that weren't allowed to be handwritten) on a legit typewriter. Messing up on those things was no fun. Ironically, as I've shifted away from handwriting over the past 15 years, I find myself having to Google things like "how many humps does a cursive M have." My elementary school handwriting teacher would be disappointed. We spent months tracing those "m"s and "n"s and every other letter to perfection.

I'll get into the digital transition more in the next chapter, but if you have a few fleeting moments, reach out to someone from a previous generation and genuinely ask them about their childhood. You'll be moved and motivated, perhaps, to apply some key learnings from what made it so magical to your child's very different childhood.

As I wrap this chapter, my hope is that we will all pause and pay a bit more attention to our history, keeping an open mind about how to apply the learnings of what made our parents and grandparents healthy and resilient.

Notes

1. Cummings, K.M. and Proctor, R.N. (2014). The changing public image of smoking in the United States: 1964-2014. *Cancer Epidemiology, Biomarkers & Prevention: A publication of the American Association for Cancer Research, cosponsored by the American Society of Preventive Oncology* 23 (1): 32–36. https://doi.org/10.1158/1055-9965.EPI-13-0798.
2. Parenting in a Tech World (Facebook Group). https://www.facebook.com/groups/parentinggeeks/posts/1525392354757466/.
3. wpxi.com (2024). Predators trying to connect with young teens using online platforms: How to protect your kids. https://www.wpxi.com/news/local/predators-trying-connect-with-young-teens-using-online-platforms-how-protect-your-kids/JTAXCLBMQJGOTKZ6NB3HT4HOSM/.

3 | Digital Transition

If I were a betting woman (and I'm not due to my conservative upbringing), I'd venture to say that this chapter will bring back many nostalgic memories as it relates to your childhood, high school and college years, and early professional experiences.

Over the next few pages we are going to dive into my personal first-hand encounters with growing up in the 90s/00s and becoming a professional in a world of always-connected tech to highlight just how unique of a position anyone born near the same time as me resides in. We are a rare bridge between two extremely different worlds, and this is one of the reasons why I believe we have the timely responsibility to educate, empower, and protect both our elders (who unfortunately fall victim to financial scams) and our children from harms no other population has experienced in the history of humankind.

Early Technology Experiences

High School

For people around my age, the first time they remember the Internet or computers being "the thing" varies greatly. Despite the fact that I went to a more resourced, private high school in a wealthy suburb of Atlanta from 1995 to 1999, we didn't have a personal computer at home like the other students on which I could research or write papers (or a printer on which I could print them out). I had to write them by hand at night and then get to school early

41

in the morning, use the on-campus computer lab, type the entire thing between 7:30 AM when it opened and 8:10 AM when the first bell rang, and pray the printer worked to print it out fast enough for me to get to class in 5 minutes or less before the second bell rang. In hindsight, I wonder if my teachers wouldn't accept handwritten papers (I had excellent handwriting so that shouldn't have been a blocker) or if I was too embarrassed to let them know we couldn't afford a home computer on which to create work.

Early Exposure to Mobile Phones

I remember when my dad, who was working in real estate at the time, arrived to pick up me and Jackie (my sister) for the weekend. He pulled up in his sick, bright blue soft-top Jeep that had a bulky new leather addition in the middle console. It was a *portable telephone* that was attached to a base with Velcro and a keypad made out of rubber buttons. The short, thick cord kept the phone on a limited tether, making it impossible to share the phone with anyone in the back seat. My mind was blown. I had so many questions. We now had a literal phone in the car, in a bag. How was this possible without a cord attached to a wall that connected to a pole that went—somewhere? I had never heard of this kind of wireless connectivity before. I was floored and greatly intrigued.

When I turned 16 and started driving (freedom!), my mom got me a cell phone for safety reasons. We used a company called Cingular Wireless that was eventually acquired by AT&T. I had a Nokia that enabled me to call people, and they could also call me.

That's it.

No texting, no games, no social media, no camera, no livestreaming. Thank God!

Eventually, when I was around 18, I upgraded to a Nokia model that could send limited text messages (by painstakingly having to press the ABC button one press at a time just to get to one of those letters or numbers) and allowed me to play the game Snake.

That was the extent of my tech usage in high school and into early college.

- I didn't have digital comparison traps constantly thrown in my face.
- I didn't feel pressured to use filters—only the occasional CoverGirl cover-up for blemishes and Maybelline mascara for special occasions in real life.

- I didn't know the real-time location of my friends, family, and acquaintances, nor did they know mine. As a result, I didn't have to deal with painful feelings of exclusion and FOMO (fear of missing out).
- I didn't measure my self-worth by my follower count, number of comments or likes, or engagement rate on content I created.
- I didn't feel pressure to take or send nude photos.
- I didn't worry about thoughts I shared in private being captured digitally and sent to the world.
- I didn't worry about predators outside of someone driving by me in a sketchy white van or approaching me at the mall (which actually happened and was terrifying).
- I didn't have to worry about measuring up to what my boyfriend at the time had seen on Pornhub because, at worst, he might have been exposed to a magazine or movie—and not explicit, graphic sexual content on demand.
- I wasn't influenced by an algorithm that sent me further down unhealthy rabbit holes. I had enough of that from pop culture and my peers.

Do you see where I'm going with this? Growing up today presents digital landmines that are invisible to the majority of adult eyes.

College and Introduction to Email

My freshman year of college is when I first got an email address—*something@ UGA.edu*—and I thought it was cool but not life-changing. I never really gravitated toward email, and it remains the bane of my existence to this day. I prefer text over email, and phone calls (or Zoom or Hangouts or Face-time) over text when possible, and in-person conversations over all of those options. My friends and I would send funny chain mail jokes or the occasional pictures since we now had digital cameras, but we didn't really use email for much. Early on, it just felt like another place to accumulate clutter with the occasional meaningful note that cut through.

Acquiring a Personal Computer

At some point toward the end of college, my frugal and very generous grandparents gifted us a brand-new personal computer (I think it was a Dell with a cool purple plastic exterior), and I signed up for an AOL email address in addition to my university email address. That's when the transition for me really set in. Seemingly overnight, I was finally able to write papers that I thankfully didn't have to go somewhere to type and print out within a tight time constraint anymore.

My eyes were opened to just how much financial means can give you an advantage to succeed—both academically and professionally. I was a bit angry at that unlevel playing field and never wanted to be without access to such incredible tools again. I was also introduced to the concept of instant messaging, a.k.a. the distraction factor a.k.a. digital multitasking thanks to endorphin spikes from gamification and notifications. I never chatted with anyone I didn't know in real life—but I do know that many of my friends would chat and flirt with strangers through platforms like AOL IM (Instant Messenger).

Early Internet and Media Usage

Early computer use meant surfing the web, learning all kinds of new information much faster than ever before, and getting into this new thing called downloading music and burning CDs. Gone were the days of having to spend $15 on a compact disc—instead, I could buy a pack of blank CDs, go on this site called Mozilla, download my favorite songs, and boom. Gifts abound for myself, family, and friends. As a child who read everything she could voraciously, this portal called the Internet with blogs and forums and articles and eventually domain names that I could buy and websites that I could build myself? It was like stumbling upon a cave full of pure gold.

Having this kind of access led to novel ways of generating income as well. I have always been crafty and would make accessories on the side to sell at local art shows. My then-boyfriend-now-husband told me about how he and his buddy Quickie bought and sold domains as a side hustle in college and lent me his digital camera, and I went to work styling, photographing, uploading, editing, SEO image optimizing, and posting my creations to my very own website. I almost fell out of my purple desk chair when I got my first online order shortly after publishing my website to the world (thank you Earthlink for building an easy web hosting/ecommerce platform that an analog kid could navigate). It was a $500 order out of Australia (of all places). For a kid living at home making $10/hour on average, this was unheard of. In fact, this was a pretty revolutionary opportunity for humanity in general—the ability to buy and sell goods online, not just in real life. If only I had invented crypto…kidding. Those orders were few and far between, but I also didn't have time to devote to building my brand full-time. I had to finish college first.

College Break

As my dad aptly warned me, the University of Georgia was a party school, and he really did not want me to attend. Growing up in two very conservative households did not fully prepare me for the freedom I would encounter while finally living on my own (in a dorm, with a roommate, but still). What I don't think he realized is that the UGA from the 80s (football, Greek life, drink all day, party all night, repeat) was (in *some* ways) much different from the UGA of the late 90s—very hard to get into and academically more rigorous. I was very proud to have worked my tail off and granted acceptance on a full scholarship to this school. So many of my hardworking friends did not get in, and I didn't take it for granted.

At first.

But given my propensity to seek acceptance from my peers at the time, I did end up succumbing to the party life that still existed, at least around the fraternities and sororities of the time—full of wealthy kids who received beaucoup financial support from their parents and didn't have to work. All they had to do was pass. And that they did—pass out every night yet still manage to also pass their classes. I couldn't maintain that lifestyle while also trying to work and pay my own way for things that the Hope Scholarship didn't cover, like books, food, gas, car insurance, clothes, medical/dental visits, and, yes, partying. My mom was super kind and helped where she could. In fact, she helped too much. It's one of the reasons I work so hard to this day—as I can never repay her for her sacrifices, but I sure hope to be able to spoil her for the rest of her life.

What happened in college and during the time I took a break from UGA is best saved for another day—or another book—but as it relates to technology exposure, it was the last peaceful break I had before being thrown into hyperconnectivity.

While on my break, I lived at home with my mom and nannied for two amazing families. I consider them to be extended family to this day.

We played outside. We read books. I took them on so many walks and adventures. We colored. We played with LEGO bricks. We had limited screen time—and when we did use screens for a break, it was *Baby Einstein*, *The Wiggles*, *Blues Clues*, or *Dora the Explorer*. The time I spent with those three children—6-month-old twins via family 1 and a 4-month-old boy via family 2—was life-changing. The ability to move from a very self-centered environment (college) to one of sacrifice and maturity (caring for babies!) helped me in more ways than I can describe here. But I am forever grateful for that time, those insights, and the parents who trusted me with their precious children and mentored me to return, finish my degree, and make big things happen in this world.

College Return

When I did return to finish my bachelor of business administration in marketing degree, I did not go back to UGA for very long. I tried at first to commute from Atlanta, Georgia, to Athens, Georgia, for classes (a little over an hour drive with no traffic)—as living there would have put me right back in some very unhealthy situations, but it was such a time-suck to balance that commute with my nannying hours, and I couldn't afford the wear and tear on my Honda Civic. So I formally withdrew and finished at a college in Atlanta, which shall remain nameless because I wouldn't recommend it to anyone. That college required you to use their very specific overpriced laptop that you could only purchase through them, and it was such a racket. I remember being baffled that we could now surf the web in class. How did they expect us to just take notes on that thing? It was unreasonable to give us that much access and expect us to fully be present in class. It still is, to this day—but I'll touch more on tech in schools later in this book. Unfortunately, and I will never forget this as long as I live because it was so traumatic, I was exposed to a live, unedited murder while on campus thanks to these laptops and very lax filters. My classmate called me over during a break and said, "You've gotta see this." It was a hostage situation overseas, and I want to tell you more so you can grasp the gravity of the graphic violence I witnessed—but I also want to spare you from any more details so I will leave it at that. My brain and heart were not ready to process that horror at age 21. They still cannot handle it to this day. Please keep in mind that our children now have access to content just like this if their parents and schools do not have adequate protections in place. Thankfully, I'll help you with that later in this book.

Internship at WSTR-FM (Star 94)

Two weeks after (finally!) graduating from college with a BBA in marketing I began interning at WSTR-FM as a national sales promotions coordinator. Known to locals as Star 94, the station was one of the top in the Atlanta area, beloved by many for decades by playing top 40 hits and staging fun, engaging, hyperlocal events all across town.

I switched from a Nokia something or other to a BlackBerry for easier texting capabilities, a better camera, the ability to email (minimally) and surf the Web on the go, and, honestly, the cool factor. Here I was, working at the local top radio station at a time where streaming platforms like Pandora, portable MP3 players, and satellite radio like Sirius XM didn't yet exist. If you wanted to listen to music, you had to tune in to the local radio stations, go to a live concert, or buy the CD or tape.

When we left work, we legitimately left work. We weren't expected to respond to emails after 5 or 6 PM because we were away from our work computers and not everyone was tethered to a mobile device that allowed us to communicate 24/7/365. Not to mention, when you work in media, it's all about networking. Evening events were where connections were made and potential clients were courted and landed via long, fun hours, lots of alcohol or cocaine or marijuana if that was your thing, and tons of IRL time. We had as much work-life balance as our social calendars would allow, and while our devices now allowed us to email without sitting at our desks in our offices, I don't recall ever feeling the urge to whittle down my inbox while tucked in bed at 3 AM.

Media Landscape Transformation

A few months into my time at the station learning the ins and outs of marketing, sales, copywriting, event planning, ad matrixes, campaign budgeting, reach, frequency, branding, schmoozing, photography, and more—the media landscape changed forever and hasn't slowed down ever since. The radio industry had chugged along without (much) disruption from 1920 to 2004—and suddenly everything picked up at warp-speed.

Evolution of Media Consumption

Within the first 24 months of my time at one of the top media properties in the top 10 markets in the United States, everything changed.

We started to direct people to "Star 94 dot com" to listen to replays of show segments and learn more about specific advertisers. We started rolling out digital offers and encouraging listeners to sign up for our email marketing lists to be the first to be in the know.

We now had to compete with not only other radio stations—but other media entities entirely. Players like Pandora and Myspace emerged, and new technology like Sirius satellite radio, MP3 players, iPods, and eventually the iPhone gave traditional radio a run for its money.

Impact on Work Culture

Digital media became a strong contender for the commodity of human attention, and we had to fight for our share of that time and the ad dollars that accompanied it. Social media was becoming a bigger and bigger player. We all sat and watched, pretty helplessly, while traditional media ad budgets were rapidly declining and digital media ad budgets were increasing exponentially. We had to pivot to maintain market share.

We also were not immune from Internet browsing on the clock and social media time sucks. It was darn near impossible to solely focus on prospecting and closing new business between the hours of 7:30 AM and 7:30 PM (yes, I was a workaholic) without taking a "quick" break to read a news article on the MSN home page or check Facebook to stalk your ex, uh, I mean, see what your buddies had been up to. To be fair, the lines quickly blurred in determining what was even on or off the clock anymore, and Star 94 absolutely got more than 40 hours a week of productivity out of me.

Remember 2006–2012, when Buzzfeed quizzes, Huffington Post articles, and Perez Hilton gossip were all the rage on Facebook? My, what a time. And that doesn't even scratch the surface when it comes to Internet rabbit holes.

Today, platforms like X (formerly Twitter), Pinterest, and Tumblr showcase some of the best, most creative, and insightful content imaginable. However, they can also expose you to some of the darkest, most depraved content you never knew existed—content so horrific that it haunts your thoughts long after you've seen it, impossible to forget.

Personal Life and Technological Impact

Starting a Family

Around March 2008, my husband Bjorn and I decided to try for our first child and by May 2008 our hopes had become reality. By January 2009 we were parents.

I'll never forget working on my personal HP laptop at night while pregnant, using this cool new thing called a VPN to dial into my office computer, wondering if the Wi-Fi or the EMFs would harm my growing son somehow. I remember asking my OBGYN about that and the look on her face. I'm pretty sure she thought I was equal parts adorable and paranoid, possibly more of the latter than the former. But I was a first-time pregnant mom with hormones doing what hormones do, and I was worried about everything.

And I had access to the Internet. And forums. And mom groups. I'll never forget learning from my colleague and fastest friend (a recent graduate of my Georgia Tech, the school my Dad wished I had attended) that Facebook had opened up its platform to everyone, not just to college students who had a college email, but everyone. Thank you, Jenny. You remain a bright spot in my life to this day.

I dove in. Especially as impending motherhood played such a big factor in my life.

Postpartum Experiences

Little did I know about the vaunted Facebook algorithm that had such power over my decision-making. I now firmly believe that the articles it showed me accelerated my descent into the exaggerated fears that frequently paralyzed me. Pesticides. Food dyes. EMFs from cell phones and towers. BPA in bottles. Bad plastic. Good (?) plastic. GMOs. Big Pharma. Vaccine injuries. Lead in toys. Lead in soil. Lead in water. It felt like the world was no longer safe and the government I used to trust to protect the public, with entities like the EPA, FDA, CDC, etc., was all a ruse. Who could I trust? Turns out it was certainly not the place where I was spending the majority of my free time: Facebook.

While never providing all the answers, Facebook did help me connect with former classmates and friends I had drifted away from. It provided hours of entertainment in the form of status updates, photos, eventually videos, and curated articles from friends and friends of friends that I was interested in. But also? It was borderline stalking and ushered all of us into an era of filtered lives that didn't "measure up."

Balancing Motherhood and a Full-Time Career

Because I thought this is what new moms do, just 12 weeks after giving birth I went back to work, crying in the prize closet that doubled as a place for breastfeeding mothers to pump.

I lasted three days back at work and decided that I had to be home with my baby, especially if I was only going to have this experience once in my life. More on that in a bit.

Despite reading *What to Expect When You're Expecting* by Heidi Murkoff and Sharon Mazel and *Breastfeeding: A Parent's Guide* by Amy Spangler, I was not prepared for the sleep torture (others call it simply "lack of sleep"—I beg to differ), the uncertainty, the anxiety, and the loneliness.

When I was that account executive at Star 94, it was so cool. So fun. So much energy. You know, Usher would stop by. The Jonas Brothers would sing to us in our Penthouse Suite conference room that towered over Buckhead. Jennifer Lopez would effortlessly glide past my desk. It was just a very happening scene at the time. VIPs everywhere, tickets to anything, seats in any restaurant.

Back then, the economy tanked (a.k.a. the Great Recession that began in December 2007), and suddenly, a dramatically reduced number of clients wanted to buy airtime—the very thing we account executives sold in 15-, 30-, and 60-second increments, earning a nice commission. The new economic conditions were tough on a commissioned salesperson, and after an impulsive last-minute birthday trip to Los Angeles to visit a friend at E!, which led to two sleepless days in Vegas, I was ready for a change.

I came home craving safety, sanity, and sobriety, and I told my husband, "I think I'm ready to have a baby now." He is a few years older than me and had been ready but, knowing I'd be the one carrying the child, was patiently waiting for me to come to terms with what that life change would mean for my body and my career.

After I had my son, I experienced a very serious bout of postpartum depression and anxiety and honestly, PTSD from the whole traumatic birth experience. It's something you really can't anticipate. For me, it came out of nowhere, in a snap. On top of that, with a very healthy pregnancy and no prior health conditions, I experienced a heartbreaking and terrifying situation during labor and postpartum that resulted in multiple doctors telling me it would be life-threatening for me to have any more biological children.

For the first five months of my son's life, I was just in a kind of fog of exhaustion and anxiety. I was always afraid. I was afraid of the stability of my physical health due to the traumatic experiences that happened in and post labor. I was afraid I would be plucked from the planet before he could even form a memory of me. I was afraid I wouldn't get to see him grow up. I would have intrusive thoughts of him getting hurt (like accidentally dropping him, or him falling into my in-law's pool), and they haunted me.

I was afraid of our environment and detested any lawn or pest company coming to spray who knows what cancer-causing chemical on our neighbor's lawn because they would inevitably make their way into our yard and air space. I was the opposite of the wild, vibrant, fun-loving Titania of my youth. I was a shell. It was so awful.

I had gone from a fast-paced, scene-y, pop star–dotted world to being at home alone, breastfeeding in yoga pants that never practiced any actual yoga, and surrounded by dishes that I had to wash extra carefully because… control what you can control, right?

How was this my life now?

Just to pour some proverbial salt into my own wounds, I would then watch people still out there living their best lives on social media. From my much different place, I was then scrolling through all of their successes, either personally (wait, you can have a baby and fit into your pre-pregnancy jeans?) or professionally. I saw their backstage celebrity moments, their appearances on this show and that show, their launching this company or that company, their having bigshot meetings with bigshot people for bigshot reasons, and their launching these cool lifestyle brands. But I wasn't doing any of that.

I was like "Life is so short. How can I simultaneously be here for these precious, fleeting moments with my son but also not get super behind in my career and non-motherhood goals I want to accomplish? The longer I'm out of the game, the further behind I'm going to be. And what's next for me professionally? Who's going to hire me? What am I going to do?" I was really in a rut but not completely hopeless.

Transition to Social Media and Freelance Work

Facebook as a Source of Income

As a new mom, I was struggling with breastfeeding in particular, and the stress was exacerbated by everything I had read online about "breast being best." Thankfully I was able to speak to Amy Spangler, IBCLC, about my specific struggles with my pain and my son's latch. Her advice changed the game for me, and I ended up successfully breastfeeding for well past the one-year mark (which was my goal).

I wrote her a letter (not an email!) to thank her for helping me and told her if there was anything I could ever do for her, to please let me know.

Wow, did I not realize what that offer would mean for my career!

Do you know how many times I have said that to someone?

"If there's anything I can ever do for you, please let me know."

Hundreds.

And do you know how many times the recipient has in fact, let me know?

Once. Just once. And this was it.

She asked me what I knew about Facebook.

I giggled—and probably said something to the effect of "Only that I spend too much time on it, why?"

It was the perfect answer as Amy created a brand called baby gooroo and was looking to utilize social media—especially Facebook—to grow that brand by publishing snippets of relevant content there and connecting with other moms.

I was perfect for the job.

I remain overwhelmed with gratitude for that connection to Amy Spangler. She was such a blessing in our lives and is an instrumental reason why I have the career I have to this day.

Starting with baby gooroo

I set out establishing a strong presence for baby gooroo on Facebook, growing the page rapidly and garnering the attention of Amy's colleagues who asked if they could reach out to me for freelance help. She said of course, as long as they didn't hire me away.

I now had two clients: baby gooroo and the U.S. Lactation Consultant Association (USLCA).

My work caught the attention of another brand that targeted moms—PeaceLoveMom—and now I had three clients.

Expanding Client Base

Eventually, I was making more money on the side than I did as an account executive at a top radio station in the country with the flexibility to nap with my son when I needed it, take him on walks and playdates, and travel whenever, wherever, as long as I had Internet. It was amazing.

Joining RedRover

In my day-to-day research to stay up-to-date on all things parenting and tech given my expanding roles, I read an article about this cool new app called RedRover.

I had found out about it via an email newsletter I had subscribed to called DailyCandy ("a daily email newsletter that provided readers with information about hip and trendy events and businesses in their city"[1]; It was later acquired by Comcast in 2008 and then laid to rest in 2014 by NBCUniversal). At the time, I signed up immediately and then started following them on all their social media accounts because naturally I'm a nerd like that for brands I love. Back in the day, being featured in DailyCandy was like the equivalent of going viral on TikTok or Instagram. It was a big deal.

RedRover was a way to find family-friendly things to do in your city and schedule playdates. GigaOm coined it a "Geo-social network for parents," which worked really well in a dense, walkable city like New York City. I didn't think much of it until a day or so later when I was leaving the Atlanta High Museum of Art's kid hour, Jackson passed out in his car seat in the back seat (because toddler life is hard), and my iPhone 4 rings.

I remember suddenly seeing a 646 area code pop up on my screen. (646 is New York City! And this was before the time when spam callers were abusing major area codes like New York City and Los Angeles, so you actually wanted to answer the phone.) I gulped and answered it. Turns out it was Kathryn Tucker, the CEO of RedRover. She had taken interest in me after seeing me follow the company social media accounts. She did some digging to find out I lived in Atlanta, and I was a social media influencer mom, and she just so happened to be looking to launch in the Atlanta market.

RedRover. Sigh. Who doesn't adore that name? I loved that game in elementary school and can even hear the sing-songy voices now chanting: "Red rover, red rover, send Titania right over." I can see myself running as fast as I could, to barrel through two kids grasping hands as firmly as possible and if you broke through, you got to take one of their teammates back to your side. If you didn't, you joined their "chain." Clearly this was a brilliant marketing and branding move on their part—and just one of the many things I loved about this startup. The website and app were super sleek. The fonts and colors, superb. The story? A single mom doing big things? Sign me up.

Insights into the Tech Startup Culture

So boom. I was now the Atlanta market manager for a startup that was based out of New York City (in addition to my other freelance work) and I was kind of losing my mind a little bit because that sounded way cooler than it was. This was the first time I was getting the inside scoop on collaborations with other tech companies that offered location-based services and talking about things like APIs, plugins, valuations, monetizing, software updates, and engineering teams.

Kathryn was also a movie producer whose ex-husband is a very well-known figure that I won't mention here, but you could do some Googling and figure it out. Anyway, it was the closest I'd ever been to Hollywood and the New York tech scene and startup fundraising in an area where I really knew my stuff: parenting + social media + the City of Atlanta. This seemed like quite an opportunity, and I was beyond excited.

Honestly, it felt so amazing to have all of this in front of me. It opened my world to an exponential number of possibilities and professional relationships that would lead to my next role as the National Community Manager for CoolMomPicks. But before I cover the rest of my abbreviated biography—let me stop and just zoom in on something I casually dropped a few paragraphs back. The freaking iPhone, you guys. This piece of technology dropped—and basically changed the game in a completely new way—so it deserves its entire section below.

The iPhone Changes Everything

While the telegraph was huge and the television, massive—this new piece of tech that could fit in your pocket changed the landscape like nothing else has before, nor since. It's something that catapulted "just" another computer company into a lifestyle brand virtually overnight.

Impact of the First iPhone

When my son was almost one, I bought my first iPhone and wow. Just woooooowwww. It changed everything. A responsive touchscreen?! If you grew up watching Inspector Gadget, or even any of the James Bond movies, you suddenly felt like a super-techy superhero who could do anything.

Open a browser? Want a compass? Need a flashlight? Check the weather? Call someone? Text someone? Send an email? Take notes? Manage a calendar?

There's an app for that.

I don't count my BlackBerry as a smartphone, because that first iPhone was such a game changer for me, and for everyone really. But, looking back, I'm aware of how dramatically it changed the way I lived and interacted with humans and nature that surrounded me. Some of my favorite smartphone photographs to this day were taken with that iPhone 4. On the flip side, I wish I could have been more cognizant of just how much of my son's babyhood and toddlerhood that I was capturing from behind the lens versus experiencing with him, and be more mindful of the information or misinformation I would casually scroll over to once I was finished utilizing the camera app.

The Role of Algorithms and Information Overload

The algorithms had my number. I was a worried first-time mom consuming content that I truly thought was educating and empowering me, but in hindsight, no mom needed that much information about vaccines and BPA and bottles and forever chemicals in basically everything in our household. I remember stumbling upon a green mattress company (Facebook ad most likely) and for only $8,000 we could have a "safe" place to sleep that wouldn't give us cancer. It was too much.

The iPhone was a game changer for those in the business of engagement.

Dr. Marci (who you read about in Chapter 1) was involved with researching and studying the early iPhones. He provides much of the story and the amazing details in his book *Rewired: Protecting Your Brain in the Digital Age*. In short, there was a lot packed into the functionality and design, as you might expect for such a revolutionary product.

"I entered the world as a psychiatrist and neuroscientist trying to study what we define as engagement. And if you ever watch any of my talks, I talk about attention to something that emotionally impacts you, leaves a memory trace, and ultimately changes your behavior. That was our definition of engagement," Marci said.

The reason Marci liked that definition is that was how the researchers were measuring attention, at the time. They could measure emotion, memory, and behavior all with different tools. He acknowledged my work as a CMO or as a marketer—how we are in the business of inducing an action or engaging people with content—that ultimately makes them change their behavior.

Marci explained how these tools were some of the most advanced on the planet at the time, like using eye tracking and biometrics and EED back in 2006. The iPhone came out in 2007. At that point, Marci was hired by a handful of companies in this space.

The iPhone was crafted with all of this early research and understanding embedded. Essentially, the affection for this product and the functionality had started the addiction.

The iPhone era had begun.

Culturally, we saw a shift as well. Technology was changing so much and enhancing the creative industry. Because of this, we saw a division emerge among groups of people—specifically in the workplace.

There was the creative class, as it's now called, which used Apple products, armed with its full slate of creative suite software that coincidentally really, really liked to work on the Mac platform. This group would be contrasted against those working on legacy systems in more traditional work positions or governmental sectors where such new technological advances were somewhat downplayed or even discouraged.

The creative industry types were quickly embracing all things Apple or Mac (from MacIntosh) versus old-school workers who preferred and stuck with the PC (or the DOS-based) personal computers using mostly the IBM platforms. The question begged "are you Mac or PC?"

It was this world, celebrating those doers who would dare to "Think Different" as Apple's early advertising campaigns would encourage, that took a great deal of pride in the machines upon which they worked. Soon, personalities like Steve Jobs became revered as geniuses or modern-day magicians with Apple new product release events becoming massive rallies with fanfare and rabid supporters. Almost like a sports pep rally. Almost.

I remember hearing an IT professional tell me point blank "I don't work on fruit." Which of course meant he didn't work on Apple hardware or within their operating systems. The idea of "cross platform" just wasn't a thing. You were either a Mac user or a PC user, which meant soon after that the marketing teams embraced this culture divide.

Apple's famous "Mac vs. PC" campaign highlighted the difference between Mac products and their fans and the old, stodgy way of the PC-based guard. Against a simple white backdrop, Apple pitted two men to represent each side against each other in a modern-day, Lincoln–Douglas type debate. The Mac guy—a younger, hipper, good-looking young man (named actor Justin Long)—took a casual and cool approach attacking the bumbling, older, and much nerdier PC-guy who had no answers and kept failing to counter Apple's offerings.

Why am I writing so much about Apple? Well, I want to highlight how when Apple first started to dominate market share of the smartphone, tablet, MP3 player, and portable computer worlds, we were all mesmerized. We had no idea the harms that were going to befall children in particular because of this revolution. I'll expand more on that shortly as unfortunately, the majority of parents still don't realize that iPhones are not the best first phones for kids. I'm not just saying that because I work for a company that sells a safer smartphone for kids. You'll see my reasoning soon.

Reconnecting with Radio and New Roles

Return to Star 94

I remember this Apple campaign so specifically because it was running quite frequently when I first started as a panelist on the Monday Morning Mom Panel, a new segment launched on, where else? WSTR-FM.

I had left the radio station in April 2009 to stay home with Jackson and figure out the rest of my life and genuinely missed my work family. My radio station colleagues really were part of my family. I frequently have dreams to this day that I am back at the station participating in some type of HR-unfriendly shenanigans and still keep in touch with many from that era, even decades later.

And so when I left to start my biological family, there was a huge gap in my heart, and I wasn't quite sure how to fill that void. Thankfully, due to the positives of social media as it pertains to the network effect, I was able to stay in contact with those colleagues, posting about what I was doing professionally, and my work family took notice.

One day Casey Tate, producer back at Star 94's Cindy and Ray afternoon show (number 1 in its spot for a solid amount of time in Atlanta—a top 10 market!) reached out to me to see if I would be interested in going live on the radio with some local celebrities, I was floored and exuberant. It felt like a homecoming.

I will forever be indebted to Casey (may his sweet soul rest in peace) as well and to Cindy and Ray for seeing my spark and giving me a chance to light it up for them and the millions of listeners that could be reached via traditional radio and now streaming via the radio station's website and our combined social media posts.

I was geeking out about the intersection of traditional and social media, and while I had no idea what was to come, I knew the scale of our reach was unprecedented.

As my work family pulled me back in, they opened a door, and I ran through it with bells, glitter, and a feather boa on (figuratively). They gave me a boost of confidence. They helped to propel the messages I was hard at work crafting to a massive audience, and while I didn't quite see what was happening at first, they identified me as a thought-leader in this parenting tech space before I even realized it and gave me a platform to do so.

It wasn't long before I had people texting and Facebook messaging me saying that they heard me on air, and it gave me life. I was able to speak in powerful, concise soundbites and offer solid advice that nobody else was sharing—at least not in my media microcosm.

I was able to help other moms in a meaningful way and at scale—and this was especially important because as a new mom—I craved intelligent advice from trusted sources. I remember what it was like to be completely overwhelmed by motherhood, clinging to any solid advice I could find, and figure out how to apply it to my child who was like no other child on the planet. So, you could say there were some variables.

Back in the day, to build community at scale, you had only a few options at your disposal—and people weren't as candid and vulnerable as they are now online. They were more reserved and so authenticity stood out—as it was rare.

The Monday Morning Mom Panel (from the station's perspective) was a chance to relate to and connect with the core demographic WSTR-FM was looking to reach—women with a HHI (that's high household income) of $100,000+ annually, ages 25–54.

That was a special time, indeed.

CoolMomPicks and Beyond

Back to my time at RedRover and the reason I needed to take on a new role at CoolMomPicks was—well, to keep it short and sweet—RedRover was running out of funding. That meant no more paycheck for me, and I really couldn't work for free at the time. Shoot, I really can't work for free now either.

However, a colleague of mine at RedRover also had this cool thing on the side (read: a very successful, highly trafficked and monetized website) called CoolMomPicks, and she knew that RedRover had no more money to pay us but *her* organization did. So we put two and two together, and soon I had replaced my RedRover income (and then some), thanks to this really cool and increasingly popular website with corresponding popular social media profiles.

But this new work/life transition did not take place with the ease at which you are reading these words right now. I was in the middle of a storm that I didn't even know was brewing.

Mental Health Struggles and Recovery

Experiencing Anxiety and Depression

I shared previously about my experience with postpartum depression and anxiety in the first few months of my son's life. Shortly thereafter the clouds temporarily parted, and I found my bearings (a great deal in part because we had more daylight now thanks to spring turning into summer), but I had done so without any prescriptions for any pharmaceutical drugs, going to see a counselor, or doing any real therapy for those postpartum/PTSD/anxiety symptoms.

Well, as expected, so many of my unresolved issues, challenges, and early-childhood traumas returned. Now, I was a mom with a young son, had a bunch of job-related and other general stresses, and was almost 33 years old. This mixture of circumstances morphed into a pretty serious new bout with depression and anxiety.

So…trigger warning for anybody who might not be in a good place to read about suicidal ideation as that's what I'm about to share with you. Feel free to skip ahead to the next chapter if you'd like to skip over this. You will not find any judgment for me as I couldn't even look at the word suicide or see a gun in a movie without being scared during that time in my life, so I totally get it.

Also, as I wrap this chapter with my very personal story, I want to let you know the reason I'm sharing it with you.

This book is not called *The Life and Times of Titania Jordan*—it's called *Parental Control*. So here's where I'm going with this.

Suicide is the second-leading cause of death in children in the United States, and *every single day* at Bark we send between 85 and 100 severe self-harm or imminent suicidal ideation alerts to parents about their kids. This story is relevant in that I want you to know I understand, firsthand, what many children today are feeling, and I empathize with anyone who is struggling—child or adult. If I can help to reduce the stigma surrounding suicide and mental health, sign me up.

So here we go. Again, if you don't want to read about suicidal ideation, now is the time to flip to the next chapter.

If you flip to the back jacket of this book, you'll see the face of someone who has contemplated suicide (me), and I want you to know that it's okay to not be okay.

I never understood how anyone would want to proactively leave this planet until 2013. There's so much to do! There's so little time! Sure, that's what I'd say today. But that wasn't always the case.

One day many years ago, I was driving my then five-year-old son home from summer camp at a sweet, church-affiliated preschool near our modest, little white-siding box of a home in suburban Atlanta. It all happened as I passed Lenox Square Mall in my silverish gold Volkswagen Tiguan—it was then that it hit me:

IT'S ALL JUST TOO MUCH AND I CAN'T.
   (*Can't what? Can't drive? Can't parent? Can't breathe? Can't work today?*)

I felt immense fear in that moment and thankfully knew what it was based on prior experiences. I was having a panic attack—but this time it was different. I hadn't been out drinking all night. There were no drugs involved (legal or illegal). I'm not sure how much caffeine I had, but most likely it wasn't excessive.

What had been happening in my life was a cacophony of intense (and stressful) life experiences that I believe depleted my body of the right balance of serotonin that my brain needed to thrive peacefully.

- I knew RedRover was failing and would cease to exist in a few months.
- A pivotal person from my past had resurfaced—and this run-in had flooded my body with emotions I had suppressed for more than a decade. It was too much back then, and it was too much at this point in my life as well.
- We were preparing to list our house because the market was finally back up from the crash of 2008, and we wanted *out*. We also didn't know where we were going to move. Yay, uncertainty!
- I had a minor outpatient procedure within the past few days that required local anesthesia. I now know to request the kind without the stimulant epinephrine (helps with faster blood clotting but also bumps up your heart rate, mimicking symptoms of anxiety).
- My husband was also going through an intense work situation at the same time. Not a good situation to be in when looking for your next home.
- I was 32, soon to be 33, and I don't know—hormones are a b★★★★, I guess?

In that moment, though, I wasn't reflecting on all of this. All I knew was that I needed help because I COULDN'T DO IT (life?) ANY-MORE ALONE.

I was 4.2 miles away from home and called both my sister and my husband. I told them each calmly and firmly, "I need you to come to the house now."

I knew something was seriously wrong. I was terrified and had a very smart, strong-willed five-year-old who depended upon me for everything sitting sweetly ignorant of his mother's concerns in the back seat. We made it home safely, and I plopped him in front of the television with a large bag of Pirate Booty (cheddar cheese puffs—but make it cool).

"Hey Buddy, Mommy's going to lie down for a bit," I remember saying to him. "Aunt Jackie and Daddy will be here soon."

That didn't faze him of course, because Sprout (on the television screen) was on. A 24/7 channel of super kid-friendly content would certainly have to do the trick at this time.

I could hear if he needed anything because the living room was right next to my bedroom, and of course I wasn't actually going to sleep.

Jackie arrived first. I had never been so relieved to see my baby sister in my whole life. She immediately ushered in a sense of calm to the room, and I felt a sense of some relief despite what I could read on her face. She meant well, but the look she carried conveyed the fear and uncertainty that comes with someone who has never struggled with anxiety or panic attacks herself looking at someone in the middle of Category 5 storm.

My husband arrived quickly thereafter.

I couldn't explain to either of them what I was thinking and feeling in the moment or honestly for a few months after the fact. All I could relay is that I was scared and I couldn't be alone. I probably looked like I had seen a ghost, when in fact, I was afraid I was close to becoming one.

I also whispered to him quietly (out of earshot of Jackie) that I needed him to take the bullets out of our gun, and hide both the gun and the bullets, in two separate places. Somehow he understood the assignment even though I couldn't elaborate and muster any more words around that subject. I wasn't able to say out loud, "I'm afraid I might get so scared that this pain and fear won't end and I will need to make it go away. Forever."

I called my doctor—Dr. James Andrews, the most wonderful psychiatrist I've ever had the honor of knowing—and whom I had been seeing since 2004. He convinced me to take a Xanax, something that in and of itself caused me a great deal of anxiety because it affects your central nervous system (Heartbeat! Brain function! Breathing!), and I have this irrational fear every time I (rarely) take one that it will kill me. How ironic.

I took half of a half of 0.5 mg of alprazolam (generic for Xanax), the emergency "oh sh★★" prescription I kept in a bedroom drawer and soon fell asleep.

When I woke, the initial intense panic had minimally subsided, but it was nowhere near gone and wouldn't be for a good 2–3 months. Over the course of the next few days and weeks:

- I could barely eat anything, and I lost almost 15 lbs.
- Our house sold in less than a week, and we packed up and moved out in less than a month. Thank you, Wade Beacham, for helping us pack a U-Haul and unpack a U-Haul in the course of one night.
- I lived in a constant state of fear, not knowing if or when I would feel that intense feeling again. It came when it wanted to, and I had to surrender knowing I was not in control.
- I needed to stay near a restroom because in me, the physical symptoms of anxiety present themselves as tummy issues (in addition to breathing and heart issues). I'll leave it at that.
- The only exercise I could do was literally a yoga class for senior citizens. I'm not joking. It was low-key, the coolest, and yet most depressing workout class of my life—had to keep that heart rate super low.
- I couldn't hear or see the word *suicide* without getting really scared. I never really understood trigger alert warnings until I needed one—also—trigger—wtf can we please use a different word?

  - **I share this with you because** I was so scared and felt so alone during that time, and if I can be a source of strength for you (if God forbid you endure something like this), I'm happy to.
  - **I share this with you because** the suicide rate in our country is on the rise—suicide is the second leading cause of death in children 10–24 years of age.[2]
  - **I share this with you because** I wouldn't be here if I didn't have access to healthcare, a strong family support system, and a flexible work-from-home schedule that enabled me to properly heal. So many people do not have that and it's heartbreaking.
  - **I share this with you because** as a child and well into adulthood, I was under the impression that anyone who committed suicide would go to hell. I no longer think that having experienced the pain that comes firsthand with not knowing if you can endure the intrusive dark thoughts, the anxiety, and the physical symptoms that manifest themselves in the body. No one can endure that for an extended period without help. Some people can't or don't know who to ask for help.
  - **I share this with you because** before I knew what I know now, I was afraid that if I mentioned my dark thoughts to anyone,

I would get punished in some way—carted away to a loony bin, deemed unfit to parent, and everyone would look at me differently from that moment forward. There would be a big "she's lost it" tattoo on my forehead.

Now I know just how many people struggle with this, and yet, the stigma remains.

I just wanted the pain to end and the fear to go away. It felt like torture—just an invisible, persistent form. I was so scared that when Dr. Andrews suggested I start on a low, daily dose of fluoxetine (generic for Prozac) my first thought wasn't one of relief. Instead, it was intense fear that if the Prozac didn't kick in (it can take up to 30 days to really start working fully), then I would really be sh★★ out of luck.

You see, I was struggling daily without meds or anything that others might use to numb the pain/calm their mind—like even a glass of wine or a marijuana joint. But because of that, there was hope. I had hope that if it got really bad, like *really, really bad*, I knew there were a ton of prescription meds on the market (thanks, television commercials) I could try and maybe it would get better. But, if I started taking them and they didn't work—oof—that was it. There was no other option. There was no hope.

I now know that type of thinking is called catastrophizing. And I don't recommend it. More often than not, your worst fears never actually materialize, and you end up wasting valuable time and energy on absolutely nothing.

Back to the really, really bad scenario—I finally and thankfully came to the realization that I was in it, almost like the eye of a storm and could not continue living in anxiety hell. Dr. Andrews explained to me that because of the recent cyclone of stress, my neural pathways had been conditioned to fast-track the anxiety in a way that if I kept trying to fight it, it might just make it worse and harder for me to overcome.

Recovery Process

He explained that if I could get my body back in balance, with the help of 10–20 mg/day of whatever comes in the little seafoam green and cream capsule imprinted with PLIVA 648 supplied by Teva Pharmaceuticals USA, I could begin to heal, before long enjoy a sense of peace, and dial my body back from fight-or-flight mode.

I picked up my prescription from CVS, my son blissfully unaware in his overpriced Recaro car seat behind me, and drove straight to my husband's office.

I was scared (what? Who, me?) to take that first pill alone, so I did it when he could be around me and watch my son if something bad happened.

We said a prayer, and I cried a little (having to take prescription meds made me feel like a failure, like I wasn't strong enough, like I didn't have the faith of a mustard seed), and I plopped that baby down my throat with some ice-cold office water.

I looked outside and, kid you not, saw the sun fighting through the clouds.

You see, that year had been the rainiest ever in Atlanta and the sun was barely out for days or maybe even weeks at a time. It was like we had moved to Seattle. Until that minute. When I looked out the window the clouds literally parted and the sun shined on my face and I felt a rush wave over me as if God was saying *baby girl, everything is going to be okay*. It was one of the most beautiful moments of my life, and I will never forget it.

It took a few weeks to feel stabilized, but sure enough, I was slowly able to live a normal (whatever that means) functioning life again.

I stopped fearing being home alone (before, I was scared to be left alone with my thoughts for too long in the event I wouldn't be able to handle it anymore and I would just have to end it all and Bjorn and Jackson would come home to find me no longer living).

I started to regain my appetite. Yay, food! I stopped having spells of uncontrollable shaking and emergency trips to the restroom. I was able to exercise again without feeling like I was going to have a heart attack. (During crisis mode, anything that got my heart rate up felt like a pounding death knell.) Being on a low dose of Prozac also helped with things that I didn't realize were a pain in my rear.

Whenever I had to fly, it no longer felt like I couldn't breathe when they closed the cabin door. That used to be ridiculously scary to me. Now, air travel is kind of, dare I say it, fun. I still clapped like an old lady on the inside every time the plane would land but no longer white-knuckled the armrest and kept my eyes locked on the flight attendants for any signs of fear on their faces any time there was the slightest bit of turbulence.

I was way more chill. Like, freshman-year-of-college chill. My germophobia and OCD subsided greatly, and I was just generally more pleasant to be around.

Today, it's a balance—I don't ever want to become numb or checked out—but overall, I've come to the realization that it's okay not to feel all the feelings, all the time, in order to—you know—survive.

Perhaps, even thrive.

Sharing Personal Stories

So now (pardon that mental health intermission, but it was so important to cover for a variety of reasons), I'm taking my Prozac, avoiding alcohol, prioritizing sleep, taking walks, and managing social media for a few additional brands on the regular. I'm also working for a well-known brand that is now literally blowing up with interest and business. And did I mention I'm working with two women who I greatly admire and are gladly mentoring me every day?

One aspect that I admired so much about these two women, the founders of CoolMomPicks, was how vulnerable they had been in sharing their own journeys with motherhood, anxiety, and depression via their blogs. These were the kinds of blogs that were much simpler—when people still wrote blogs that weren't full of sponsored content. It was a time when people still read blogs online instead of scrolling aimlessly through Instagram for hours at a time.

Eventually, this led me to KidsLink. KidsLink began as an app that would offer parents and caregivers the ability to share documents, photos, and moments safely within their circle—be it grandparents, school, camp, or babysitters.

While CoolMomPicks was an amazing opportunity—it was part-time consulting, and I was juggling multiple clients, motherhood, and mental health—what better next step to take than to go back to work full-time with a (drumroll) startup!

(I am being facetious here, just in case that wasn't clear.)

Continued Professional Growth

KidsLink and Privet

KidsLink initially reached out to me to consult on their social media strategy—and what's the saying? That escalated quickly. And it did, in an amazing way. It was my second go with a startup, my first time being back in a full-time position, but this time was different.

The world had shifted (slightly) to embrace the flexibility that a working mother needs—allowing her to give her best but in dedicated, focused spurts. It was incredible to be on a team of parents working on tech that sought to keep families connected and protected.

From there, we spun out a very popular social media platform called Privet. That landed me on *The Today Show*. It was nuts, and in addition to that the local Atlanta NBC affiliate 11ALIVE asked me to try out to be the new host of the weekend tech show, *Atlanta Tech Edge*. I didn't take a single broadcast journalism class in school and had never read from a teleprompter, but I gave it my absolute all and got the part. It was one of the most thrilling calls I've ever received in my life—from then Executive Producer Chris von Seeger.

So many incredible yet tough things were simultaneously happening in my life—busting my rear as the CMO and co-founder of Privet (a startup with zero revenue) full-time, hosting a tech show in a top 10 media market, being a mother, managing mental health—and in the midst of it all Brian Bason, the CEO of Bark and dad of two boys who took a big risk leaving Twitter to launch a company that keeps kids safer online, saw me on a national TV outlet (*The Doctors*) and reached out via LinkedIn. The rest is history.

It's the best job in the entire world, for me at least, because it doesn't feel like a job. It's a mission.

And that leads me to where we are now.

Joining Bark

I (almost) swore to myself that I would never join another startup again. Like, ever. But there was something very different about Bark Technologies, Brian Bason, the mission, the team, and the technology—and if any startup was going to make it, it was this one. Given that 9 out of 10 startups will fail according to multiple sources including Forbes,[3] you really need to feel good about working for one if you are going to take such a risk.

Conclusion

So why did I just spend the past 17,000 words or so recounting my personal and professional history circa 1995–2024? Well, we (those born within a decade or so of 1980) have a unique responsibility to inform, equip, and protect both our elders and our children from the unique challenges of this digital era—challenges no other generation has ever faced. Because my generation experienced life both before and after the digital revolution, we really are the hope of the future until our children can mature enough to educate and protect us even further.

But we have to safely and effectively get them to that point first.

Reflections on the Journey

What stands out the most to me as I think back to how technology did or did not play a role in my formative educational and professional years is how passive it was. It really was an afterthought that, until now, I couldn't look back on with clarity and see just how revolutionary it truly was.

Looking Ahead

So what's next? You have patiently sat with me while I told you a great deal about myself, and if you didn't already skip ahead by now, wow, and thank you. Now it's time to switch the narrative and focus on you, your family, your community, what you need to know, and what you can do about it. Let's get into it.

Notes

1. Wikipedia (2024). DailyCandy. https://en.wikipedia.org/wiki/DailyCandy.
2. National Institute of Mental Health (n.d.). Suicide. https://www.nimh.nih.gov/health/statistics/suicide#:~:text=Suicide%20was%20the%20second%20leading,ages%20of%2035%20and%2044.
3. Patel, N. (2015). 90% Of Startups Fail: Here's What You Need to Know About the 10%. *Forbes.* https://www.forbes.com/sites/neilpatel/2015/01/16/90-of-startups-will-fail-heres-what-you-need-to-know-about-the-10/.

4

Where We Are Now

So, where are we now when it comes to technology? In short, it's a staggering, wonderful, terrifying, exciting, frustrating, beautiful, and absolutely horrific place. If we are to examine all of the stats and facts, here in the middle of the 20s, and take a snapshot of what's happening around children, parenting, and technology, the information is fairly astounding. Technology's influence is everywhere. This chapter will serve as the reflection, a snapshot to give us an idea of where we are now. We will look at the effect tech has at home, in school, and on the playground itself. It's all interconnected, of course.

We are in the middle of a great awakening, where parents, legislators, tech executives, scientists, teachers, doctors, young adults, and therapists are sounding the alarm surrounding the harms that have specifically impacted children as a result of too much unprotected tech, too soon—and in a few chapters (Chapter 9 to be exact) we will review what our future options look like. We are at a crossroads, and there are two distinct paths that clearly present themselves if we pay attention. But before we get to "The Solutions" (Chapter 8) I need to make sure you are crystal clear on the current state of children and technology.

That's what this critical chapter aims to do, as concisely as possible. It will be hard for some to hear the truth that lies within, but we cannot effectively make lasting change for good until we know what we are fully up against.

So what should we be paying attention to? What has changed? What's not normal?

Look at the Data

Placing numerous anecdotes and personal parenting experiences aside for a moment, it's always a good idea to start with any data points you have. Given that we at Bark Technologies have been surfacing alerts to parents, caregivers, school administrators, and—in certain life-threatening situations—law enforcement since 2015, I am uniquely positioned to share some of that data with you now.

Just over the course of 2023, Bark analyzed more than 5.6 billion messages across texts, email, YouTube, and 30+ apps and social media platforms on behalf of families.

Keep in mind before you read these that each data point represents **a child**. There's extended family or a friend circle or a community involved who are dealing with life's toughest issues.

From our report, "Kids have complex digital worlds, and these activities represent late-night DMs, urgent texts with friends, and comments on countless apps—places where children communicate the most frequently. Bark's software monitors these conversations in places where parents may not even know to look."[1]

The percentages for each category represent the number of Bark users who were sent alerts when their child engaged with or encountered a particular subject matter.

Here are just some of the eye-opening and gut-wrenching stats we surfaced:

Self-harm/Suicide: 33% of tweens and 57% of teens were involved in a self-harm/suicidal situation.

Sexual Content: 58% of tweens and 75% of teens encountered nudity or content of a sexual nature.

Anxiety: 19% of tweens and 36% of teens used language or were exposed to language about anxiety.

Drugs/Alcohol: 58% of tweens and 77% of teens engaged in conversations surrounding drugs/alcohol.

Bullying: 67% of tweens and 76% of teens experienced bullying as a bully, victim, or witness.

Depression: 26% of tweens and 38% of teens engaged in conversations about depression.

Disordered Eating: 9% of tweens and 21% of teens engaged with or encountered content about disordered eating.

Predators: 8% of tweens and 10% of teens encountered predatory behaviors from someone online.

Violence: 68% of tweens and 82% of teens expressed or experienced violent subject matter/thoughts.

Due to my role as chief marketing officer (CMO) and chief parenting officer at Bark, I am constantly faced with a barrage of both data and heartbreaking stories in my DMs about some of the darkest behavior on the web.

Both the software and hardware options we offer analyze the rate at which children are in harm's way due to technology, including how often they struggle, which platforms are the most problematic, and what issues are increasing in frequency year over year.

Every time I share these stats, and it is multiple times each week as of writing this, it hurts. It centers me. It shakes the audience when I present on stage or through Zoom (as it should). But you don't just need to hear it from me.

It's now time to hear from some experts as well as personal stories from parents, children, and law enforcement officials.

Childhood 2.0

Whenever I speak to groups large or small, what precedes the stats you just read in my token presentation is a 2-minute and 21-second trailer for a documentary called *Childhood 2.0* that will rock you to your core.

Some quotes from the powerful film that reinforce where we are today[2]:

> "We also know that the teen suicide rate increased 56% (last year alone)."
> —*Dr. Patty Agaston*

Suicide is the second leading cause of death today for children, adolescents, and young adults, ages 10–24, according to the American Academy of Pediatrics.[3] At Bark, we are sending (on average) between 85 and 100 severe self-harm and suicidal ideation alerts to parents and caregivers **about their children each day**.

Every. Single. Day.

"I can just scroll for hours on end."

— *A young teenager*

We will get to screen-time nuances shortly, but—*hours*. Each day. Hours that could be spent on so many other, more worthwhile pursuits. Hours that are not spent moving their bodies, reading actual books, connecting with peers in real life. It's so sad.

"It's actually a way we can keep track of them in the real world where things really are scary."

—*A mom*

Sure, you can track your child's location in real time thanks to smartphones, and don't get me wrong, that absolutely delivers peace of mind in many instances. But, if that smartphone doesn't have the proper controls, filters, time limits, and monitoring, the virtual world (I would argue) is actually much scarier.

"The lives of kids were sort of changing slowly for a while, and then all of a sudden those kids were able to get on social media, and that's when everything skyrocketed."

—*Dr. Free Hess, emergency room physician*

I'm not sure words can do this scene justice. You really have to watch the graph of the explosion of social media apps jet up and to the right—and overlay that with the rate at which tweens and teens experienced a sharp rise in issues surrounding their mental health. You don't have to be a scientist to see the correlation.

"Last year we received over 18 million reports of international and domestic online child sexual abuse."

—*John Clark, former president and CEO of the National Center for Missing & Exploited Children*

The sexual exploitation and predation of children is on the rise. The Federal Bureau of Investigation (FBI) released multiple warnings about sextortion, particularly in teen boys. "From October 2021 to March 2023, the FBI and Homeland Security Investigations received over 13,000 reports of online financial sextortion of minors. The sextortion involved at least 12,600 victims—primarily boys—and led to at least 20 suicides."[4] Victims of this particular crime tend to be 14–17-year-old boys, but anyone can be a victim of this type of crime. Additionally, at any given moment, there are approximately 500,000 predators, "scrolling through social media platforms, gaming apps and chat rooms, trying to connect with kids."[5]

This is a jarring reality that every parent and caregiver needs to know.

> "We have traded a false sense of safety and security for actually putting our kids in riskier situations."
>
> —*Chris McKenna, ProtectYoungEyes.com*

Let's hover on this quote for another moment. Let this sink in.

We have parents who are afraid to let their kids explore the real world solo but have no issues giving them digital access to the entire world (and the entire world to them) within the walls of their "safe" home.

> "Well, yeah, like, nudes of girls go around the school all the time."
>
> —*A young female teenager*

The way she says this—so nonchalant—is heartbreaking. These are children, and this type of media distribution is illegal—much less damaging to reputations, relationships, and mental health.

> "There were men that wanted to talk to children at all hours of the day and night."
>
> —*Me, in reference to our work posing undercover as children on Instagram*

At Bark, we went undercover as an 11-year-old on Instagram and within minutes had adult men arriving in our DMs looking to video chat (or worse) live. I'll never forget the sound of one man's voice in particular. He says through a thick, faux "calming" accent, "Don't be shy." It still makes me nauseous to this day.

> "Right now, we're effectively living in an experiment. How is this going to affect us? We'll find out."
>
> —*Dr. Joel Stoddard*

This is the quote that the *Childhood 2.0* directors decided to end the trailer on with some escalating, dramatic music, and it really hits home. It never fails to give me chills when I hear it (and I hear it at least once a week). They are not wrong. We still don't know the outcome of giving our children, with their developing hearts and brains, too much access, too soon.

So we have multiple anecdotal situations giving us "on-the-ground" proof of what's happening to our children.

We have multiple, credible experts across a variety of professional fields telling us what they are seeing and it's not good.

We have severely outdated laws that haven't been updated since before the majority of these apps and these devices existed, and legislators debating, for too many years now, what to do about it—meanwhile every single day more children are harmed.

We have…to do something.

Screen Time

Children today are spending upward of eight hours a day online—between school and home use.

> One study of more than 1600 children in the USA tracked screen use trends from 2015 to 2019. It found that children aged 8–12 years used screens for entertainment for an average of 4 h and 44 min a day. The figure for those aged 13–18 was 7 h and 22 min a day. Screen time for schoolwork and homework was added to those figures. The data that are available also suggest that a significant proportion of toddlers uses digital devices for more than an hour a day. This goes against the World Health Organization recommendation of no screen time for children under

2 years of age and less than an hour a day for those aged 2–4 years. Interestingly, a 2014 study estimated that parents use digital media for an average of 9 h/day. It also raises concerns about how technology may interfere with interpersonal interactions or the time parents spend with their children.[6]

Some say we've reached a tipping point in technology consumption. Others say we've just scratched the surface. However, what we do know is that the business of technology is a massive one. We also now know what technology does to our brains, our bodies, and our spirits. We see it anecdotally every single day. There are stories of hope and hurt, and stories from halfway around the world and right next door. It's what brings us together and unfortunately can tear us apart.

I was scrolling on Facebook recently (shocker), and I was floored to see a post in a mom's group from a grandmother asking for show recommendations for her three-month-old grandson.

I repeat: **her three-month-old grandson**.

Accompanying her text-based post was a video of a fresh, tiny infant who was about the same size of the smartphone that was thrust in his face, lighting up his eyes.

You can literally see the smartphone screen reflection in his glassy eyeballs—the fast rate of frame changes, the brightness levels varying faster than he would experience in real life by studying nature or his grandmother's face. My heart sank. I wanted to scream at my laptop.

I wanted the ability to reach through my screen and swat that phone out of that grandmother's hand and break that baby of his trance-like state. My heart broke for what I envisioned was happening in his brain—and for the lack of knowledge that persists around the risks of exposing young children to stimulating screens too early. I really wanted to leave a gentle comment, but I decided against it.

How could I possibly explain in a nonjudgmental but firm way just how bad it was without starting a fight in the comments? Maybe she truly didn't know the negative consequences of what she was doing.

But most of us do. Most of us have an inherent understanding that babies and toddlers shouldn't have screens inches from their faces. It doesn't take any of this hard data to support the concept that only at a certain age is it even considered okay to give a child any type of screen.

Screens Are Just the Tip of the Iceberg

Unfortunately, this is a world where common sense and inherent understanding isn't always a given. I pulled a few concerning headlines and sub-headlines involving children that we as a society wouldn't have even been able to fathom we would be dealing with a few short years ago:

- "How One School Made a Deepfake Porn Incident Worse"—*Forbes*[7]
- "Francesca Mani told her mother she would not be a victim after fake images were circulated around her New Jersey school"—*The Guardian*[8]
- "On popular online platforms, predatory groups coerce children into self-harm"—*The Washington Post*[9]
- "Sextortion: What Kids and Caregivers Need to Know"—The FBI[10]
- "Mother shares how she discovered app predator used to coax her child into producing pornographic images"—KDSK NBC St. Louis[11]
- "Social media harms teens' mental health, mounting evidence shows. What now?"—*Science News*[12]
- "Hunting Utah's biggest bully — social media"—*Deseret News*[13]
- "Surgeon General Issues New Advisory About Effects Social Media Use Has on Youth Mental Health"—HHS.gov[14]

Do your eyes start to gloss over as you read the headlines? Or do some of these, any of these, hurt your heart as they do mine?

We are just getting started; there's so much more. Many parents show up to my talks or Facebook Group looking for advice around screen-time limits, when in reality, screen time should be the least of their tech worries (in context—it's still a huge issue and needs to be addressed but in comparison to the harmful content and people that children encounter while having their screen time, it's a lesser evil).

My son Jackson even wrote a piece for me to share what he thought most parents aren't aware of today:

> Video games promote child gambling in the forms of loot boxes, pack openings, and many more methods. especially in games like NBA 2K and Apex Legends where kids tend to spend hundreds on these packs and loot boxes and test their hand just like they would at a slot machine.

In NBA 2K, players can purchase packs and hope to get certain player cards from these packs. The contents of the packs vary but a player will hope to pull one of the most expensive and valuable cards (dark matter or galaxy opal) and when a player pulls one of these expensive cards they can sell them on a virtual auction house in the game. And there are even many websites where you can sell the virtual currency you obtain from selling these cards in exchange for actual money.

It is literally just child gambling. Players will often spend hundreds of dollars on these packs and lose a lot of money. It is the same case with the loot boxes in Apex Legends. There are actually loot boxes in many video games but in the case of Apex Legends it is one of the more extreme cases. It is essentially just a slot machine where players will spend hundreds on a 1 in 500 chance of getting an "heirloom" (a super rare cosmetic item) but the catch is that every apex pack that you open, the 1 in 500 chance will increase.

For an example, if you bought 20 apex packs for $20 then your chances would increase to 1 in 480, and so on. This incentivizes players to just spend more and more and more until you get the chance low enough to obtain one of these heirlooms. Some more examples of games that include gambling are many different Roblox games, FIFA, Star Wars Battlefront 2, and many more. These loot boxes are literally designed to be addictive and result in millions of kids gambling and losing their money.

Oof. The self-awareness of a kid at that age blows me away, and the addictive nature of these games breaks my heart for kids who don't realize what they are getting into.

In addition to the typical parent worries like "When will my child learn to read?" or "Should I reapply sunscreen?" we now must talk to our children about some of the hardest and most mature aspects of humanity, much younger than previous generations, and more frequently than we might think.

So. Many. Apps

In addition to paying attention to how much time we spend on screens, we need to look long and hard at the problematic content and people our children encounter daily through tech.

The majority of these concerning encounters take place through the apps we "allow" our children to download and utilize. That is—if we have turned on the app approval setting.

Some are categorized as social media. Some are not. Some live under the guise of games or even productivity—but almost all have a social component that allows for two-way communication with both friends *and* strangers as well as the sharing of media (images, videos, GIFs, emoji, and disappearing chats).

Once you realize that these apps, games, and websites our children use are portals to the entire world and allow the entire world to access our children, you start to see things in a new (darker, but more realistic) light.

The Worst App

Let's talk about the most popular app with kids today. Crapchat.

I'm sorry. I meant Snapchat.

In short, Snapchat encourages the sharing of disappearing media—which in a vacuum can be extremely fun and harmless, but not once it reaches the general public.

With more than 750 million monthly active users (as of February 2023)[15] and no public data shared around how many of these users are children, we have to rely on Pew Research Studies and the like to give us that data. Sixty percent of U.S. teens ages 13–17 use Snapchat according to one recent Pew study titled "Teens, Social Media and Technology 2023,"[16] which equates to roughly 15 million U.S. teens using Snapchat daily.

According to a *TechCrunch* article from May 12, 2012, titled "No, Snapchat Isn't About Sexting, Says Co-Founder Evan Spiegel" Spiegel (its CEO) is quoted as saying, "…most user feedback from direct emails and Twitter posts is about sending funny faces and messages, not racy images. But he added that the app was partially inspired by the Anthony Weiner scandal and a desire to create an app with expiring data."[17]

Mmmkay. And let's not forget the app's original name was Picaboo. And its purpose was not to be a hide-and-seek app for infants. It was to facilitate fleeting, momentary glimpses.

So, we can see how that would quickly spiral, especially in the hands of less mature, less technologically savvy brains that aren't fully developed until they are in their early twenties.

Snapchat is also a breeding ground for location-based bullying and exclusion. Snapchat offers Snap Map inside its app, sharing the real-time, live location of its users to anyone they are connected to unless they decide to toggle on "ghost mode." Here's just one anecdote from a dad of 15-year-old twin girls who are feeling the firsthand effects of Crapchat:

> Teenagers have figured out how to weaponize Snapchat's Snap Map feature in a rather obscure way.
>
> Teens found that they can gather in-person (IRL) and use the Snap Map, not only to brag about the people that they are physically present with, but as an exclusionary tool to also identify and isolate individuals for not being at a particular event.
>
> It's the new "you're not invited to my party," but now everyone knows instantly via geolocation on Snap Map.
>
> Alternatively, teens gather for an event and then proceed to disable Snap Map, even further isolating those not invited. Surprising or not, teens know exactly when five of their friends assemble in a physical location and then all mysteriously disappear on Snap Map.

Snap Map is not only problematic for the potential fear of missing out (FOMO), stalking, and predation aspects of that feature, but it facilitates the drug trade. Kids are solicited daily and can have drugs delivered to their home as easily as a pizza within minutes.

Take the case of Sammy Chapman. "On February 7, 2021, a drug dealer reached out to our Sammy on Snapchat and delivered drugs to him at home. He snuck out after his parents were asleep to meet the dealer, who gave him what turned out to be a lethal dose of fentanyl. Fentanyl is a synthetic opioid twice as addictive as heroin, 100 times more powerful than morphine—and fatal even in microscopic doses. Sammy had no idea he was taking it. As a result, Sammy lost his life."[18]

Sammy's parents and other advocates are now working hard to push for Sammy's Law, a law I staunchly support, which would give parents the choice to use third-party safety software for their children. If Sammy's parents would have been able to use Bark with his Snapchat account, they could have been alerted to the drug deal and Sammy might still be here today. But Snapchat has refused to work with safety solutions like these, while allowing more and more kids to be harmed on its platform.

According to Paul DelPonte, executive director of National Crime Prevention Council (NCPC)—you know, the organization behind our favorite furry detective, McGruff the Crime Dog®—22 students die each week in the United States due to fake pills laced with lethal amounts of fentanyl.

This is a huge problem and social media platforms like Snapchat are making it worse.

Not only does Snapchat facilitate the sharing of presumed disappearing photos and videos, drugs, and humans for sale, it's also a place that holds dark searches and secrets behind an aptly titled feature called "my eyes only" where the absolute worst can remain hidden until it's too late.

It's not just Snapchat that's problematic, however. It is, in fact, the app I feel is the single-worst app for our kids today, as you'll see reiterated in the Q&A section toward the end of this book.

There are other areas where we are facing some dramatic and alarming issues related to our children—and remember, we will get to solutions, I promise. Those are coming in Chapter 8. But I need you to understand where we are before we can get to a better place. So let's press on.

The Business of Social Media

Did you know the top social media platforms generated more than $11 billion in ad revenue just from children alone in 2022?[19] That's big business. Not only are these companies not incentivized to keep children off their platforms, they generate revenue from them. These are for-profit companies incentivized to do everything possible to keep people on their platforms, regardless of their age, as long as possible. Don't be fooled by their public service announcements (PSAs), safety centers, and blog posts. They do not want you to take a break. Their business will suffer if enough of us do so.

These social media platforms use algorithms designed to surface the most compelling content that they deem the person viewing the content wants to see because they already know what they're interested in. Why? Well, because they tell them directly and indirectly—whether it's filling out information in a profile, the groups they belong to, friends they have, and, of course the ads they click.

We are the product (the fish if you will), and the algorithm is the hook with some tempting bait hanging off. More on that in a second. For now, just know that there's a very planned reason why my feed looks different than my husband's feed, and his looks different than our son's, which looks very different from my mother's.

We all have different interests, and whether it's Instagram, TikTok, YouTube, Pinterest, you name it, they want to keep us engaged within their platform for as long as possible because they can then charge advertisers more money for that time spent in app and they can report strong metrics to their shareholders and to their board and get a pat on the back and sweet bonuses. It's so important for our children to know how these platforms work and how these platforms are making money from them.

In addition, they are collecting troves of data—more data than we can possibly imagine. The reason they can charge so much for selling access to our eyeballs, emotions, and wallets is because they know us to our core based on what we search, what we hover over, the location proximity and frequency to others they are also tracking, and who we DM (and how often). It's the epitome of a puppet master analogy—"a shadowy, metaphorical agent that controls from behind the scenes, manipulating people and things like a puppeteer operating a puppet."[20]

The CEOs of some of the biggest tech companies—Meta, TikTok, Snapchat, X (formerly Twitter), and Discord—have all been dragged in front of Congress saying things like "Hey, our platforms are pretty safe to use for kids over 13, and we've put safety measures in place." What exactly are those safety measures? They are not very robust. I can tell you that firsthand as a parent trying to use them with my own savvy son.

Some (not all) social media platforms and games have rolled out parental controls, family safety centers, or family pairing features that may sound great on the surface through their press releases or well-designed landing pages, but when you dig into them, you realize they don't provide nearly enough critical insight for parents and caregivers to keep their children safe.

Ineffective Safety Measures

Sure there are some that are decent, and I will say that something is better than nothing, but we have certainly seen over the past half decade that very few social media platforms have done enough to try to keep vulnerable populations safe. In Chapter 8, "Solutions: So What Do We Do?" you can find out more information on the steps you can take to limit the information these companies have access to, for you and your children.

For example, Snapchat will let you know who your child might have been communicating with, but it shows you the username, not their actual name. And what it doesn't let you do is turn off Snap Map, which shows your child's real-time location down to the very granular level of what the building looks like to anyone they're connected to.

That's not okay, and as a parent, you should be able to turn that off, full stop.

Also, who are we kidding thinking kids are ready for all that these platforms have to offer at 13?

Would you let your child at that age fly solo across the ocean to another country and tour it for six months, only sending them funds along the way and FaceTiming occasionally?

Of course you wouldn't. Abso-freaking-lutely not.

Why are we outsourcing parental control, parental care, content moderation, and critical parental oversight to these companies? This is not okay.

With TikTok (and Snapchat too), they say they offer family pairing, family sharing parental controls, but your child, a minor, has the ability to unlink and disconnect from the parent account without parental consent. What is the point of it then? It's smoke and mirrors, my friends.

There's no PIN password protecting setting changes. Children can be served the option to have a private account, but they can just switch to have a public account. And in what universe and what world would it be okay to leave it up to children to decide what's in their best interest in the face of addictive, harmful content and people? That's not the kind of world any of us imagined we'd be raising our kids in one day. Yet here we are.

Algorithms Are Black Holes

Algorithms are more powerful than most of us realize, that is, unless you were part of the team that designed them for a platform. Our children don't know they're lurking behind the scenes or, frankly, how they work. Honestly, the majority of adults are easily sucked in to apps, games, and feeds, just like matter that exists anywhere near the event horizon of a black hole cannot escape its draw, not even light.

Most apps purport to be free—and sure, you might be able to download and sign up for them without exchanging any monetary currency. However, there is absolutely a cost. We all pay a steep price for the time we can never get back, the attention we lose to things that matter, the toll that the content takes on our mental health, and the lack of physical activity that negatively impacts our physical health.

Algorithms aren't inherently evil, but we are currently lacking critical oversight of what decisions humans at the largest tech companies are making as to what content is being served, at what rate, to children and adults. Much like addictive, harmful substances like cigarettes and alcohol now contain warnings labels thanks to the awareness efforts of scientists and healthcare professionals, our current U.S. Surgeon General Dr. Vivek Murty has called for social media to contain a health warning label as well.

In a piece published in June 2024, Dr. Murty states, "It is time to require a surgeon general's warning label on social media platforms, stating that social media is associated with significant mental health harms for adolescents. A surgeon general's warning label, which requires congressional action, would regularly remind parents and adolescents that social media has not been proved safe."[21]

There are multiple stories of children who have been pushed further and faster down toxic rabbit holes than if they had not spent time on certain platforms.

Algorithms mean that, unfortunately, children who are just curious or potentially struggling will stumble across subject matter that they might be curious about or wrestling with, and then that's what the majority of their feed starts to encompass.

According to the 2023 *Wall Street Journal* piece, "TikTok Feeds Teens a Diet of Darkness," by Julie Jargon, "Self-harm, sad-posting and disordered-eating videos abound on the popular app."[22]

Another damning headline from a 2021 *Wall Street Journal* piece, by Georgia Wells, Jeff Horwitz, and Deepa Seetharaman, titled "Facebook Knows Instagram Is Toxic for Teen Girls, Company Documents Show," uncovers how Meta downplayed the teen mental-health issues within its platforms.[23]

Algorithms are also responsible for exacerbating the already problematic issue of predators online looking to groom and abuse children.

Don't believe me? Take a look at any "momfluencer" account where she has posted content of her children dancing, modeling outfits, frolicking at the beach, demonstrating cheerleading routines—and then look at the comments underneath.

While you might see innocent and sweet notes from other moms or family members that this momfluencer actually knows, you will also see comments from creepy adults. Grown men are served these accounts in their feeds as "accounts you might want to follow based on your interests"—and grown men are also served minors in their "suggested accounts." A thought-leader in this space that I highly encourage you to follow is Sarah of @ mom.uncharted (her pinned hashtag says it all: #kidsarenotcontent) as she highlights some of the worst stories that should be surfaced (and accounts that should be taken down). Momfluencer accounts are posting Amazon links in their bios to allow these predators (or these consumers of child content) to buy gifts and outfits for their minor children in the hopes that those children will then display those outfits online. Instagram and other platforms should absolutely be shutting this down. These children cannot consent to that display of their digital footprint, and it's outright disgusting.

Unacceptable algorithms further foster the connection of harmful accounts to children (pedophiles and criminals looking to participate in sextortion).

The fact that these platforms either know a child's actual age or know that a child is around a certain age based on what they're searching for, the language that they use, and the contacts they're connected to—and yet still surface to them adult people and adult content, whether it's through suggested contacts or content that they show in their feed—is outright unconscionable. Not only is it unacceptable, but it should also be illegal. But the laws meant to keep children safer online have not been updated since I was in high school. That was, unfortunately, way too long ago—before TikTok and Instagram were even a twinkle in their creators' eyes.

Paul Raffile is the canary in the coal mine when it comes to this issue. He was hired by Meta to help combat sexual exploitation of minors across their platforms (Facebook, Instagram, and WhatsApp), and after leading a webinar to bring global players together to fight this trend, he received an email from his hiring manager at Meta informing him that the offer had essentially been rescinded.

Before he was even able to get started.[24]

He stated in his viral LinkedIn post that garnered multiple millions of views globally:

> 🔥 Meta fired me before I even started.
>
> 🔎 Meta recruited me to lead their Human Exploitation investigations. My job was to prevent real-world harm from crimes like sextortion and trafficking. I was supposed to start Monday.
>
> 🔪 But moments after hosting a webinar to combat the surge of sextortion targeting minors, and hearing from the parents of children who were killed by this crime, I got the phone call rescinding my offer.
>
> 💡 Meta sought my expertise after I exposed how cybercriminals are using a vast network of fake Instagram accounts to blackmail tens of thousands of teens with sextortion schemes, driving dozens of victims to suicide.
>
> 🚫 Yet they rescinded the offer evidently for this same exact reason. Feels like retaliation.
>
> I'll be okay…
>
> But the tens of thousands of people currently being exploited on Meta Platforms won't be.

That ended up being a blessing in disguise in my opinion—as it showed the true colors of the (lack of) value Meta places on child protection, and now Paul's efforts are having an even larger impact. Multiple social media platforms have now implemented his impactful suggestions, and Instagram just recently launched teen accounts, a new type of "safer" account that all children 16 and under will default into starting around early November 2024. It's not enough, but it's something. Not ironically, Instagram released this child safety update one day before a Senate Committee Hearing on this very topic, looking to add more regulations to social media platforms to reduce the rate of child harm. Any discerning human can see this was a PR play, more smoke and mirrors to deflect from the actual culpability at hand.

As I mentioned earlier in this chapter, the top social media platforms generated more than $11 billion in ad revenue off children (it's so staggering it bears repeating), some of whom aren't even supposed to be on those platforms unless they're 13 years or older.

Remember, that algorithm, because it isn't taking into account that child's mental or physical health, will show them more of that content leading children down dark rabbit holes, and it can exacerbate already existing mental and physical health issues.

General Safety

Back in the day, a predator had to physically be in the same location as a minor to cause harm. Children were safe at home (outside of problematic family members), and the risk existed in the real world as predators could lurk at the playground, ball field, church, camp, or mall.

Now, the estimated half a million predators who are known to be online at any given time know that the Internet is a vast playground of children who are online upward of eight hours a day. Most predators know how to talk to children, coerce them, and pressure them to send nudes and or meet up in real life. I'll never forget sitting at the Child Rescue Coalition headquarters in Florida looking at two very jarring things:

- A live, global map of all of the known addresses where child sexual abuse material (CSAM) lived
- A user manual hundreds of pages long outlining how to groom and abuse a child, step-by-step, as created by a network of abusers and shared far and wide

As I've interacted with thousands of parents over the years on this exact subject, a common theme that has emerged is one of fear surrounding letting their children roam as they (adults) were able to when they were younger. What's ironic about that is kidnapping rates seemed to have decreased since the 80s—thanks to rapid advancements in safety and law enforcement technology.

According to Reuters, "Fewer than 350 people under the age of 21 have been abducted by strangers in the United States per year, on average, between 2010–2017."[25] Contrast that with the sheer number of strangers that we enable our children to interact with daily online.

Even places like Pinterest and Roblox (and even places that say they don't allow it) are still infiltrated by predators. In 2019, our team at Bark Technologies created a persona, an 11-year-old girl, and went undercover on Instagram (and a few other platforms), and within minutes we had grown men reaching out to us for inappropriate reasons.

We endured this grueling work to show the public just how quickly this can happen and that it absolutely can happen to your child. Please don't think "not my child." And the rate at which predators are trying to reach out to children online is through the roof. It's very, very scary and problematic, and according to Detective Rich Wistocki, a retired child cybercrimes expert based in Illinois, the average predator has 250 victims over the course of their lifetime and "One of the greatest risks to our children are the devices they carry with them every day."

Here's a quick story about Kaylee, another undercover persona we created at Bark. As a "14-year-old" (as it said in her bio), she began to garner serious interest and not just from peers her age. A grown man who self-identified as being 41 years old in the United Kingdom was messaging her (us), attempting to groom her by pressuring her to communicate, send photos, and appearing to care about her safety and saying things like "I don't want any funny business and make sure you do good in school, make sure you don't get caught with your phone." He sent a disappearing photo to us at one point as we were filming with ABC in NYC, and the tension in that room was so high as Jodie, my brave colleague, said, "Ready?" She clicked the picture, not knowing what it would be. Thankfully, it wasn't a full nude but a shirtless photo of this man, who by the way also happened to be a dad (he claimed). We all sighed a collective mix of relief that it wasn't a full nude—but also shared disgust that we were even on the receiving end of this type of media. We reported this account to Instagram, but it remained active for at least six months after reporting. Meanwhile, he never stopped asking for pictures and updates and even created other accounts and tried to follow us from those accounts as well.

The ease and speed at which an adult man was able to connect with a 14-year-old persona and have persistent chats that, if we engaged with long enough, had some pretty disturbing things to surface still baffles us to this day.

These horror stories continue ad nauseum. And it is nauseating.

Thankfully, I discuss strategies that parents can use to protect their children from this sort of predation in Chapter 8, "Solutions: So What Do We Do?" as well as throughout Chapter 12, "Resources."

Sexting and Nudes

This leads me to sexting. I'll never forget speaking to a group of middle school parents at a local Atlanta faith-based private school and the principal wanted to know if my presentation covered sexting because as she put it, "Titania, sexting is the new first base."

That was a gut punch.

And outside of the relational and reputational issues surrounding the distribution of nude media of minors, there are real, legal ramifications for this behavior. Every state has different laws on the books, but in general, the possession or distribution of nude media of anyone under the age of 18 is against the law. Period.

Children are being pressured to send nude pictures of themselves. Nudes. Children are receiving nudes even against their will if they have features like Airdrop set to Anyone or Everybody for Ten Minutes. Essentially, if they have an iPhone without the right settings implemented, people can and will just drop a nude to your child if they are out in public.

It's pretty jarring, but it's so important for children to know that sending, forwarding, or receiving and saving a nude photo or video of anybody under the age of 18 to a digital device is distribution or possession of CSAM.

There are legal ramifications for having or sending CSAM, and that can result in prison time for people under the age of 18. In many states, this also results in having to register as a sex offender. These are real, life-alerting, college- and career-ending consequences, whether you intended to possess this material or it was a mistake.

Now, are children actually being prosecuted frequently for this? No, but there are some states that will make an example of some children, and nobody wants their child to be such an example, right?

We hear stories daily of children who sent a nude photo to their boyfriend or girlfriend thinking that's where it would end (or that it would disappear because they sent it through Snapchat, Instagram, or WhatsApp). But unfortunately, it doesn't end. Remember, the Internet is forever. If that image becomes shared and it circulates within peer groups, teams, schools or wider communities, it can continue to spread like wildfire. Even disappearing photos live on a server somewhere, in a deleted photo album for 30 days, or as a screen shot or digital photo taken of a screen as to not alert you that a screenshot has taken place.

Not only does this kind of situation affect them socially, but deep mental health issues may develop. An image of a child naked can ultimately have serious and lasting impact on their reputation, their attendance in school, and their grades. In some cases, this can have a staggering, dark, and cascading effect on all aspects of their lives, their parents' lives, their friends lives, and so many other people in their circles. It's utterly heartbreaking.

If this does happen, there are some steps to take that I outline in Chapters 8 and 12. Of course, empathy here is key. There is no need to shame or grow angry despite the anger or betrayal you may feel. There is no doubt that they are often already suffering so much, and we need to help them figure out what to do next.

Like I said, the Internet is forever. Once any image is uploaded, there really is no telling how fast and how far that image will be shared across the universe. Regardless of the reason and regardless of what that picture is, once it's accessible to anyone online, it will be accessible to everyone online. And while there are some companies out there that try to find and limit the proliferation of images, there is really no way to prevent them from being spread—only exhausting efforts to take them down. The cost (financial and emotional) to try to have those pictures removed can be staggering.

For example, Erin Andrews, a popular broadcaster, fell victim to someone taking a peephole video of her changing in, what she thought, was the safety of her hotel room. She took the person who violated her privacy to court, was successful in finding justice, and then spent a fortune working to find any and all places where that video was housed. Clearly, it is a lesson for us all.

The scary thing is, these images and videos don't have to be uploaded to become vulnerable. There are instances where private phones are hacked and images are shared every day. Every few years we hear about other celebrities who have had their private information stolen off their phones or, in most cases, from someone's private iCloud or online photo storage.

The stolen imagery from a known, popular figure generates interest due to their clout, and the information is spread across social media. Then that stolen property becomes monetized to make money for those hosting or holding them. They are also used as blackmail where the thief or hacker will seek staggering payments not to spread, send, or release the images…but only for that moment or that payment.

But, it's not just celebrities who are targeted. Anyone who has had a lost or stolen phone can fall victim to someone gaining access to private photos.

In fact, in a recent conversation with Aniko Hill, co-founder of DopaMind, a nonprofit organization working to teach kids and their caregivers, parents, and teachers about how to navigate modern technology and empower them to make brain-healthy media choices, we discussed the proliferation of this type of abuse media.

It's bad enough that we have to deal with the actual existence and distribution of CSAM online and that we have to help children understand the problems with sending nudes. But now, we must also confront AI-generated explicit photos and videos of kids that steal their likeness. Children are now also being abused by someone putting their face on an AI-generated model. It's heartbreaking because they still feel shame and embarrassment, and it is devastating as it still impacts their mental and physical health. This is why I strongly encourage all parents and children to have *private* accounts if they are going to share photos of themselves online. If you post public photos of your face to the Internet, anyone can grab that photo and turn it into a false, damaging narrative.

A 2024 piece published in *Pediatrics* titled "Rising Threats of AI-Driven Child Sexual Abuse Material" covers "the production and dissemination of virtual child sexual abuse material (VCSAM), which poses imminent risks to pediatric and adolescent populations."[26] This piece also goes on to state that "In 2022, the National Center for Missing & Exploited Children's CyberTipline received ~32 million suspected reports of online CSAM alone. Moreover, studies have reported significant upticks in the amount of circulating VCSAM and researchers foresee cases rising dramatically...."

Now thankfully, not to jump ahead to solutions because those are coming, but I might as well mention that the National Center for Missing and Exploited Children (NCMEC) now has a helpful site called Take It Down where you can get the help you need, if God forbid, your child has been exposed to this experience or is a victim of this. It's also important to know that every state in the United States has an Internet Crimes Against Children (ICAC) unit, and they are there to help your family.

So if you are worried about your child's online interactions—whether you suspect they're talking to an adult, sharing or receiving inappropriate photos or videos, being extorted or sextorted, or even being bullied—you can reach out to your state's ICAC unit. They have seen everything and help families just like yours.

Cyberbullying

Hurt people hurt people. Not every bully needs the police called on them, as certain instances of childhood teasing is just a rite of passage and can help build empathy and compassion within those who are the target.

On the flip side, if you as an adult have tried to put an end to the bullying that is happening, whether it's by reaching out to the parent of the child who is the bully or going through the school and it's just not stopping, sometimes you do need to review the laws of your state to see what power you have to make this stop. Because it is not okay. Period.

Nobody, especially a child, should ever be the target (victim) of bullying. And sometimes you do need to resort to legal options to make that stop because it affects their mental and physical health long-term.

The number of children who encounter bullying, and bullying itself, today is much different than in the past. Children used to be able to go home and escape it, but now if they have a device with them, they can't escape it. It follows them; it haunts them.

They're being bullied and they're being doxxed (having their personal information published online without their consent). Bullying can also look like exclusion. For example, sometimes children will create text threads and then kick one child off the thread to pointedly exclude them as an act of bullying. Another form of exclusion that we mentioned earlier surfaces in features like Instagram's "Close Friends" and Snapchat's Snap Map.

I've spoken to Rose Bronstein, mother of Nate Bronstein, who will forever be 15. According to my conversations with her, and the nonprofit Buckets over Bullying launched to honor his memory and prevent this from happening to other children, "Nate's bright future was cut short on January 13, 2022, when he died by suicide after facing severe cyberbullying by his peers. A group of classmates and basketball teammates at the Latin School of Chicago harassed and threatened Nate through a JV basketball group text and Snapchat, with one of the messages cruelly directing him to kill himself."

This, unfortunately, is just one of many heartbreaking stories that we hear daily at Bark, and we have to work collectively (and urgently) to combat the rise in this issue. Children are telling other children to go kill themselves. Some are joking. Some are serious. It's unimaginable, but it's so very real and pervasive.

Overprogrammed

In an effort to keep our children engaged and out of harm's way, we've left no room for them to simply figure it out. Packed after-school and weekend schedules abound. Books and lessons have moved from paper to screens. It's nuts.

Look at the race for summer camps that now begins in January in certain circles. Parents are collectively so scared that kids will spend their summer days on screens as opposed to down at the creek or at the gym or at the swimming hole or playing outside until the streetlights go on so they opt to pay thousands of dollars to send them away for weeks at a time to a screen-free outdoor retreat. I don't blame them.

Obviously, there's a practical side of having kids under the supervision of a competent adult while a parent attends to things like, you know, work so they can make money and live. But how much nonparental supervision is too much? What happened to the play-based childhood?

Can children be bored? Is it okay to be bored? If they're really bored, will they find trouble?

Is all this a fair assessment of the state of children's daily lives? Isn't this all about balance? Can downtime exist without a screen? And how can kids learn how to wind down without a screen?

These are among the questions that parents are faced with in today's world.

The iPad is not a trusted babysitter, but it has become the most popular form of childcare. Most parents think it's a harmless way to get a quick shower, a few moments of peace, a nap perhaps, or an interruption-free conference call. I get it. I've been there.

But it's not teaching our children how to cope with boredom (which is actually good for kids by the way) or respect parental boundaries. We are numbing and pacifying them with one of the most addictive creations known to human civilization. That should alarm all of us.

Education in the Information Age

"Technology should be utilized as a tool to encourage true inquisition for information but not as a sole information provider," high school alternative program coordinator and principal LeighAnne Terry said. "Similar to a tool in a mechanics toolbox, it doesn't fit everything but does work for many things and should be utilized for effectiveness with proper oversight."

When I needed to decompress during school, I would draw on my notebook while still listening to the teacher. When I wanted to interact socially with my peers, I had to wait until a break in class: in-between classes, lunch, recess, or after school. Then, once we were able to engage with each other, the rush of joy and excitement would carry you like a skilled surfer riding the very best wave over to a group of humans with which you would make eye-contact and engage for as long as they allowed before it was time to focus again.

But that was then; this is now. At some point it became acceptable to allow easily distracted children to bring portable supercomputers into their classroom and blatantly engage with them over listening to the teacher or each other—even after being forced onto screens for the duration of their school day.

In their school years, children are being introduced to more and more technology at school, and there's unbelievable pressure to use more. In some ways, it feels like Google, Microsoft, Lenovo, Apple, and other edtech companies are fighting for the classroom just like they fought for the personal computing market, right? They benefit when more devices are sold—regardless of who will be using those devices (children) and what harms may come as a result.

Yet, LeighAnn, a professional educator for more than 22 years, doesn't see screen use as all negative, if doled out responsibly. It can be used as an engaging and compelling way to deliver information.

"Technology-driven lessons in education can inadvertently contribute to teacher burnout and retention issues," LeighAnne said. "Most people go into teaching because they value building relationships and making an impact. When interactions with students are primarily through a screen, it can reduce the sense of connection and fulfillment that teachers rely on to stay motivated."

LeighAnn explained to me what she noticed when each student was first granted a device for school in a "one-to-one initiative" at South Carolina public schools.

"We immediately started seeing more of an increased reliance on screens as the primary educational delivery system," she said. "The students' dependency and access to information first centered on their devices rather than true learning and retaining information through teaching methods."

The principal explained how this inquiry model began as a welcome sense of true individual-seeking information for understanding. However, over time the novel aspect of it lost its luster, and they found students stuck in front of screens, messaging each other within the same room and missing out on chances for true human interaction. This eroded social skills so much that conflict and misunderstandings became more complex.

Simply put, students were not picking up on basic social cues. Using screens throughout the school day yielded more apathy and lack of motivation. Additionally, they did not help students who struggled with focus and did not have intrinsic motivation to complete so many competing tasks and overcome distractions with or without district firewalls (the browser and Internet access limitations that so many schools create).

She contends that personal cell phones and connected devices like watches contribute greatly and now are the number-one systemic factor to lack of focus, lost engagement, and challenging social interaction for adolescent students.

Many parents don't realize that school-issued devices and accounts are putting children at risk as well. My own research revealed that only about 60% of the school-issued tech in the United States has the appropriate filters and management on it to protect kids just while they're on campus, much less if they can take them home. We are giving our children so much access without the proper safety tools to help them use it safely.

Caroline Gebhardt, as a mother of school-age children, has experienced firsthand how her children in different grade levels and school environments have had various screen usage, just as curriculum content varies. She also works with those "elders" in schools along with parents at home to help students become curious in using screens in responsible, information-seeking ways. The key is responsibility.

She has seen how schools use screens as downtime or pseudo-recess, especially on a regular basis, and how this practice becomes yet another way students can become disembodied, with a tendency to dissociate, decreasing capacity for executive functioning and focus.

She's advocated on behalf of her children for increased playtime in schools as well as pointing to the science that supports it—and that most of us have known intuitively for generations.

"Studies show the importance and value of play and movement as paths toward intrinsic motivation and healthy brain development," she said. "As we as a culture—within education and home life—become more dependent upon screens as a way to pass time or due to a lack of resources, we unconsciously rob the next generation of exploring various ways of being present and attuned to their appetite for life."

How long is recess now? How long was recess back in the day? If my memory serves me correctly, we had at least an hour *during* the school day to move, run around, climb, and free play, not to mention another hour of physical activity year-round in a class literally called *physical education*.

According to the State Policy Database, only 9 out of 50 U.S. states require recess.[27]

According to the Georgia Department of Health (my home state),

State Board of Education Policy (1110-6) requires the Department of Education to establish regulations or guidelines for physical activity. All public school must provide students in all grades with at least 20 minutes a day of supervised recess, during which schools must encourage moderate to vigorous physical activity. Schools do not use physical activity as a punishment nor withhold opportunities for physical activity as punishment.[28]

Two things really stand out to me from that excerpt:

- "At least 20 minutes a day"—goodness that's not nearly enough. It takes five minutes just to get the children to the outdoors or area of play and five minutes to get back to the classroom. So, that really ends up being just 10 minutes of play each day allocated to children. Unacceptable.
- Recess should not be withheld from children in any circumstances. In other words, do not dangle losing recess over a child's head as a potential punishment. Goodness knows it's children who act up most in class that most likely also are the ones who most need that movement, physical activity, and unstructured free play time.

Today, children in many public school systems are lucky if they get 20 minutes of unstructured movement—but national standards state that "Children and adolescents aged 6 to 17 years should have 60 minutes or more of physical activity every day."[28]

Caroline has spoken directly to schools and school systems about her desire for the education system as a whole to become more trauma-informed as well as a massive push for more recess in every school her children have attended. Without fail, the response has been that the faculty and staff agree and desire such changes—the policy makers refuse it. And ultimately, we see less and less recess.

Along with asking for more movement in schools, she hopes to help change policy to equip the schools with more polyvagal knowledge (how the way our bodies feel and how that can impact our emotions) and arming more staff with training and education that emphasizes the value of relationally informed instruction and learning.

According to the National Institute for Health, "the polyvagal theory proposes that the evolution of the mammalian autonomic nervous system provides the neurophysiological substrates for adaptive behavioral strategies. It further proposes that physiological state limits the range of behavior and psychological experience."[29]

Slowing down the pace of pushing kids ahead, developing more critical thinking regarding the achievement-oriented culture, and better understanding behavior as communication as well as nervous system functioning will be key in helping the next generation to reclaim a more sustainable path toward education, learning and growth, Gebhardt believes.

There is, however, a growing movement to get smartphones out of schools, but surprisingly, parents seem to be the biggest blocker of this coming to fruition. According to journalist and author Abigail Shrier on episode #2109 of *The Joe Rogan Experience* (podcast),[30] this began about eight years ago (in 2016). This movement really picked up steam with the release of Jonathan Haidt's *The Anxious Generation* (if you haven't heard of his book, yet somehow landed on this book, I have so many questions but let's table that), and more schools started the 2024–2025 school year with "away for the day" policies. This is a big win!

Silicon Valley executives send their kids to Waldorf schools. Why is that? What do they know about screens that we don't?

Well, clearly something. And many parents feel the same way. Just pay attention to the number of Waldorf or similar nature-based modalities that have grown in popularity as digital learning, and subsequently the necessity of online or asynchronous learning (as many school districts now call teaching class on Zoom), has grown.

While the founder of Steiner schools, and ultimately Waldorf, Rudolph Steiner had long passed before even the advent of television, he knew that childhood was a time to be, well, children. In fact, to this day, the motto of the Waldorf School of Atlanta has "Childhood First" painted in large, colorful letters across its marketing materials. Without going into detail about the Waldorf philosophy, the school tailors its unique curriculum around anthropology, nature, and eurythmy—or body-based mindful movement.

Here's an example: as children begin to become exposed to numbers, they collect different elements from the outdoor world to identify the number. For example, a three-leaved clover is collected to represent the number 3. Or a tulip poplar whose trunk splits into two segments is associated with the number 2.

Human evolution is incorporated as the study of different global cultures, beginning with the indigenous populations. As grades progress, lessons correlate the teachings, discoveries, and ways of people living in the Stone and Bronze ages; the Egyptian, Norse, Persian, Arabian, Chinese and Indian civilizations; and ultimately the Greek and Roman ages.

And guess what? None of those brilliant cultures used an iPad! But that was then, and this is, well, this is where we are today.

Waldorf insists upon a media-light school experience and also makes families pledge to fulfill the same guidelines at home. It's a requirement for enrollment. In theory, Waldorf school children won't get home from school and plop down to game or watch TV for hours upon end. Weekends are not to be binged on *Fortnite* or *Roblox* or the latest Netflix special. Real-world results do vary, however.

According to the Association of Waldorf Schools of North America (AWSNA), a nonprofit membership organization of independent Waldorf schools and institutes in Canada, the United States, and Mexico:

Waldorf teachers appreciate that technology must assume a role in education, but at the appropriate developmental stage, when a young person has reached the intellectual maturity to reason abstractly and process concretely on his or her own, which is at around the age of 14.

Society might challenge this principle, as many young children are well able to complete sophisticated tasks on a computer; the Waldorf perspective is that computer exposure should not be based on capability but on developmental appropriateness. While many applaud adult-like thinking in young children, we observe that a child's natural, instinctive, creative and curious way of relating to the world may be repressed when technology is introduced into learning environments at an early age.

I appreciate that technology must assume a role in education, but at the appropriate developmental stage, when a young person has reached the intellectual maturity to reason abstractly and process concretely on his or her own, around the age of 14.[31]

In short, screens have no part in a Waldorf curriculum in the early grades but may be introduced in Waldorf high schools, when appropriate and always for research, classwork, presentation, or other common-sense practices.

Administrators long for the days of loud lunchrooms and noisy hallways where students would interact with each other in-person instead of through snaps. When districts returned to school full-time after students returned to in-person school from a virtual school hiatus, we saw students who were unable to interact peacefully and bullying increased exponentially.

Only a few years out from the return to the classroom post-pandemic, the lunchroom chaos has returned—but it's so much different now in schools that have not gone screen-free. Children are filming fights instead of trying to stop them.

We Are in the Thick of It

To answer the question this chapter first posed, where are we now? Well, my friends, we could not be deeper in the depths of a collective "What have we done and how do we get out of it?" revelation as a society.

We have administrators who have lost control.

We have parents who have lost control.

And while none of us is ever really in control—hence the tongue-in-cheek name of this book—we have options and critical decisions to make.

Notes

1. Bark (2023). What being online was like for kids in 2023. https://www.bark.us/annual-report-2023/.

2. Muratore, R., Winans, J., and Winans, K.K. (Directors) (2020). *Childhood 2.0: The Living Experiment [Film]*. Double Edge Films.

3. American Academy of Pediatrics (2024). Suicide: pediatric mental health minute series. https://www.aap.org/en/patient-care/mental-health-minute/suicide/?srsltid=AfmBOooJK86MKslIXILMslpyp NJh1Y3FmEZjQv0gwblpT-QhlQsSmTtj.

4. Clement-Webb, E. (2024). Sextortion: a growing threat targeting minors. https://www.fbi.gov/contact-us/field-offices/memphis/news/sextortion-a-growing-threat-targeting-minors#:~:text=If%20you %20or%20someone%20you,visiting%20tips.fbi.gov.

5. Johnson, D. (2024). Predators trying to connect with young teens using online platforms. How to protect your kids. https://www.wpxi.com/news/local/predators-trying-connect-with-young-teens-using-online-platforms-how-protect-your-kids/JTAXCLBMQJGOTKZ6NB3HT4HOSM/.

6. Korhonen, L. (2021). The good, the bad and the ugly of children's screen time during the COVID-19 pandemic. *Acta Paediatrica*. https://www.ncbi.nlm.nih.gov/pmc/articles/PMC8444888/.

7. Farivar, C. (2024). Teen boys deepfaked her daughter then the school made it worse one mom says. *Forbes*. https://www.forbes.com/sites/cyrusfarivar/2024/03/13/teen-boys-deepfaked-her-daughter-then-the-school-made-it-worse-one-mom-says/?sh=42aae02a3118.

8. Laughland, O. (2024). Staying silent? Not an option': family takes fight against deepfake nudes to Washington. *The Guardian*. https://www.theguardian.com/technology/2024/mar/12/family-takes-fight-against-deepfake-nudes-to-washington.

9. Boburg, S., Pranshu, V., and Dehghanpoor, C. (2024). On popular online platforms, predatory groups coerce children into self-harm. *The Washington Post*. https://www.washingtonpost.com/investigations/interactive/2024/764-predator-discord-telegram/.

10. FBI (n.d.). Sextortion. https://www.fbi.gov/how-we-can-help-you/scams-and-safety/common-scams-and-crimes/sextortion.

11. Byers, C. (2023). Mother shares how she discovered app predator used to coax her child into producing pornographic images. *ksdk.com*.

https://www.ksdk.com/article/news/investigations/predator-used-phone-app-child-sexual-abuse-material/63-812505a5-4832-46a2-a92f-00072ff5d444.

12. Gupta, S. (2024). Social media harms teens' mental health, mounting evidence shows. What now? *ScienceNews.* https://www.sciencenews.org/article/social-media-teens-mental-health.

13. Benson, L. (2024). Hunting Utah's biggest bully — social media. *DeseretNews.* https://www.deseret.com/utah/2024/03/10/social-harms-campaign-aimee-winder-newton/.

14. U.S. Department of Health and Human Services (2023). Surgeon General Issues New Advisory About Effects Social Media Use Has on Youth Mental Health. https://www.hhs.gov/about/news/2023/05/23/surgeon-general-issues-new-advisory-about-effects-social-media-use-has-youth-mental-health.html.

15. Perez, S. (2023). Snapchat announces 750M monthly active users. *Tech-Crunch.* https://techcrunch.com/2023/02/16/snapchat-announces-750-million-monthly-active-users/.

16. Anderson, M., Faverio, M., and Gottfried, J. (2023). Teens, social media and technology. *Pew Research Center.* https://www.pewresearch.org/internet/2023/12/11/teens-social-media-and-technology-2023/#:~:text=TikTok%2C%20Snapchat%20and%20Instagram%20remain%20popular%20among%20teens%3A%20Majorities%20of,%25)%20and%20Instagram%20(59%25).

17. Gallagher, B. (2012). No, Snapchat Isn't About Sexting, Says Co-Founder Evan Spiegel. *TechCrunch.* https://techcrunch.com/2012/05/12/snapchat-not-sexting/.

18. Organization for Social Media Safety (2024). Sammy's Law. https://www.socialmediasafety.org/sammys-law/.

19. Brownstein, M. (2024). Harvard study is first to estimate annual ad revenue attributable to young users of these platforms. *The Harvard Review.* https://news.harvard.edu/gazette/story/2024/01/social-media-platforms-make-11b-in-ad-revenue-from-u-s-teens/#:~:text=Social%20media%20platforms%20Facebook%2C%20Instagram,Chan%20School%20of%20Public%20Health.

20. Dictionary.com (n.d.). Puppet master. https://www.google.com/search?q=puppet+master+analogy&oq=puppet+master+analogy&gs_lcrp=EgZjaHJvbWUyCQgAEEUYORiABDIICAEQABgWGB4yC

ggCEAAYgAQYogQyCggDEAAYgAQYogQyCggEEAAYgAQYo-gTSAQgzMjIxajBqN6gCALACAA&sourceid=chrome&ie=UTF-8.

21. Chapman, M. (2024). Tobacco-like warning label for social media sought by US surgeon general who asks Congress to act. *The Associated Press.* https://apnews.com/article/surgeon-general-social-media-mental-health-df321c791493863001754401676f165c.

22. Jargon, J. (2023). TikTok feeds teens a diet of darkness. *The Wall Street Journal.* https://www.wsj.com/articles/tiktok-feeds-teens-a-diet-of-darkness-8f350507.

23. Wells, G., Horwitz, J., and Seetharaman, D. (2017). Facebook knows Instagram is toxic for teen girls, company documents show. *The Wall Street Journal.* https://www.wsj.com/articles/facebook-knows-instagram-is-toxic-for-teen-girls-company-documents-show-11631620739.

24. Raffile, P. (2024). Meta fired me before I even started. *LinkedIn.* https://www.linkedin.com/posts/raffile_meta-fired-me-before-i-even-started-activity-7192095001290395651--aXt/.

25. Reuters (2019). Kidnapped children make headlines, but abduction is rare in U.S. *Reuters.* https://www.reuters.com/article/us-wisconsin-missinggirl-data/kidnapped-children-make-headlines-but-abduction-is-rare-in-u-s-idUSKCN1P52BJ/.

26. Krishna, S., Dubrosa, F., and Milanaik, R. (2024). Rising threats of AI-driven child sexual abuse material. *Pediatrics.* https://publications.aap.org/pediatrics/article-abstract/153/2/e2023063954/196409/Rising-Threats-of-AI-Driven-Child-Sexual-Abuse?redirectedFrom=fulltext.

27. State Policy Database (n.d.). *Recess.* https://statepolicies.nasbe.org/health/categories/physical-education-physical-activity/recess.

28. Georgia Department of Public Health (n.d.). A model elementary recess school policy for school districts in Georgia. https://dph.georgia.gov/sites/dph.georgia.gov/files/Model%20Elementary%20Recess%20School%20Policy_FINAL.pdf.

29. Porges, S.W. (2009). The polyvagal theory: new insights into adaptive reactions of the autonomic nervous system. *Cleveland Clinic Journal of Medicine.* https://www.ncbi.nlm.nih.gov/pmc/articles/PMC3108032/#:~:text=SUMMARY,of%20behavior%20and%20psychological%20experience.

30. The Joe Rogan Experience (2024). *Abigail Shrier* (Podcast). https://podcasts.apple.com/us/podcast/2109-abigail-shrier/id360084272?i=1000647262501.

31. Amico, B. (2014). Other skills should take priority over coding. *The New York Times.* https://www.nytimes.com/roomfordebate/2014/05/12/teaching-code-in-the-classroom/other-skills-should-take-priority-over-coding.

5 | Digital Effects on the Brain

"While the reward-seeking parts of the brain mature earlier, the frontal cortex—essential for self-control, delay of gratification, and resistance to temptation—is not up to full capacity until the mid-20s, and preteens are at a particularly vulnerable point in development."

—*Jonathan Haidt, from* The Anxious Generation

We've just extensively reviewed where we are in terms of parenting and childhood in an uber connected world. Before we can get to the solutions, we need to go a bit deeper now from the surface level of what we are seeing externally in society to what's happening from a physiological and psychological standpoint in our bodies.

Once we (and our children) have more education and understanding surrounding how technology impacts us, then and only then can we truly make effective change.

Over the next three chapters, we will cover the top research-backed impacts that screens have on our brains, bodies, and mind/spirits. My hope is that through age-appropriate conversations with your children, you will collectively learn how to moderate screen usage (and the contents within) much like we as a society (try to) moderate our consumption of sugar.

Now as mentioned in the chapter-opening quote, the prefrontal cortex is the front part of the brain that sits behind our forehead and our eye socket. When I speak to groups of parents and children, I refer to the prefrontal cortex as the part of the brain that's responsible for impulse control, decision-making, and emotional regulation. It's an important (understatement) part of the brain.

We can use many metaphors for it, but let's go with the metaphor that Dr. Carl Marci (who you first read about in Chapter 1) uses. Essentially, the prefrontal cortex is the conductor in our brain symphony. It helps orchestrate the different brain regions, and it helps create the harmony of our ability to take in information and use it for productive lives.[1] It can also get very tired.

The brain has limited capacity and differs as the organ itself grows. Looking at the brain's relationship with technology and learning, he said that through a neurobiology and neurodevelopmental lens, "You have to think from a parenting perspective about what stage your child is at developmentally to then make recommendations about any technology because you have to understand whether the brain is capable or not."[1]

Dr. Marci gave a few examples of what he meant by this, but there were two that really stood out to me around development and finding what's relevant for a developing brain to take in: video content and reading.

This chapter starts with excerpts from my lengthy conversation with Dr. Marci and continues by discussing the hidden elements of tech interaction with our brains that we don't always focus on, and should, if we are to be mindful about our family's tech usage. By the end of this chapter you'll have a good grasp of how digital technology affects the brain. Don't worry, in Chapter 8, "Solutions: What Do We Do," I'll cover what you can do to help your children navigate this terrain.

Early Exposure to Video

According to Dr. Marci, the American Academy of Pediatrics recommends no video content whatsoever prior to age two, but he says by age three exposure to video content is okay. The reason for that is what's known as the *video transfer deficit*. What is that? Well, the video transfer deficit refers to the inability of child's brain, up until age three plus, to transfer information from a two-dimensional screen and apply it to a three-dimensional world. That would make sense, right?

An exception to this is FaceTime or video calls with family members—so please don't feel guilty for handing a screen to your child so they can chat in real time with a grandparent. Just make sure to keep those calls short and sweet, and make sure you are sitting beside them so they aren't navigating away to other applications.

In the early 1990s, one company took parenting (or, video babysitting) by storm. A young mom in her basement with a video camera and some socks started creating videos for her own babies. Julie Aigner-Clark, a former teacher, started the Baby Einstein Company because she wanted to expose her children earlier to music, art, and poetry. I was not yet a mom at this time, but I do remember seeing TV segments about how, somehow, exposing your children to classical music in utero would result in a child with higher IQ points. It sounded plausible, but how would I know? There was no Google yet. Something must have been going around education circles at the time that would encourage this type of thinking because at some point during that period, one out of every three households with a child under the age of three had at least one Baby Einstein video.

Parents would marvel about how long their babies could sit there and watch those videos. Well, in 2007 the *American Journal of Pediatrics* came out with a study that showed that there was, in fact, a direct correlation with the amount of time you spend watching Baby Einstein and *regression* in learning.[2]

Not only were these kids not getting ahead, but they were also falling behind. And that's when researchers started to say, well, why is that? It's because their brains are just not developed enough to watch something on TV and make sense of it in the real world.

Importance of Nonscreen Reading

Reading was invented by humans about 5,000 years ago. So before that, we didn't sit around reading books. We didn't have books, but we had the same brain. We are not born with specialized neural networks in our brain dedicated to reading. It is a learned skill that pulls multiple brain regions together. You must have vision, language, attention, and comprehension at the minimum to process it all.

Reading takes thousands of hours to actually master as a skill. When you look at the brains of three- to five-year-olds who spend a lot of time consuming video and not a lot of time in front of a book, their reading network—which you can now measure with brain scans—is just not as robust. Kids who consume a lot of videos without reading have lower overall comprehension. They're falling behind. So, when they're three to five, make sure your kids are reading actual books.

I asked Dr. Marci if e-books were any better. His answer was interesting. "Well, believe it or not, studies have been done on that subject, too," he said. "The problem with electronic books, ebooks, is what is called haptics. Haptics is the feeling of holding something: turning the page, looking at progression, and not spending time pushing buttons. What the studies show is that kids get caught up in technology and they lose the story. And what's important is the reading and the story—the comprehension suffers."[1]

The Top Impacts of Technology on the Developing Brain

It's time to get into the nitty-gritty, keeping in mind that I am neither a doctor nor a scientist. I am a voracious reader and complier of data from those much smarter than I. Here's what I found.

Decreased Attention Span and Memory Retention

With the rising rates of ADHD among children today, we have to look at the variety of factors that might be contributing to it—whether environmental or, perhaps, due to better testing and more awareness of the diagnosis. In fact, according to the *Journal of Clinical Child & Adolescent Psychology*, "Pediatric ADHD remains an ongoing and expanding public health concern, as approximately 1 million more children had ever received an ADHD diagnosis in 2022 than in 2016."[3]

What cannot be argued is the fact that frequent use of screens has been linked to a reduced ability to maintain focus, especially due to rapid switching between activities.[4] Context switching even for adults is hard, and introducing distraction factors for children early on cannot be ideal for their ability to focus.

On the topic of diminished memory recall, an insightful piece in *Science* states that, "…when people expect to have future access to information, they have lower rates of recall of the information itself and enhanced recall instead for where to access it. The Internet has become a primary form of external or transactive memory, where information is stored collectively outside ourselves."[5] In essence, our over-reliance on digital devices to recall information reduces the need for memorization and weakens long-term retention.

Improved Problem-Solving Skills

Note, this is a positive! As you read this book, I want you to keep in mind that tech is neither good nor bad. Tech is a tool that needs to be used responsibly. Much like I'm using a MacBook Air to write this book to help educate and empower all of you, technology when used in the right context for our children can be a positive.

According to Marc Prensky, author of *Digital Game-Based Learning*, video games and educational apps can foster critical thinking and enhance problem-solving abilities in children. Now he goes as far to say that "Video games are not the enemy, but the best opportunity we have to engage our kids in real learning."[6] I think that's a stretch, but something we should consider as a complement to traditional learning methods. Many are concerned about how the lightning-fast availability of answers through search engines may discourage deeper cognitive processing and critical thinking when solving problems—so perhaps this one is a net zero (neither positive or negative).

Increased Multitasking, Decreased Productivity

Smartphones give us the ability to do so much, but at what cost? According to the National Library of Medicine, "Results showed that heavy media multitaskers are more susceptible to interference from irrelevant environmental stimuli and from irrelevant representations in memory. This led to the surprising result that heavy media multitaskers performed worse on a test of task-switching ability, likely due to reduced ability to filter out interference from the irrelevant task set."[7] The takeaway? Children who regularly switch between apps or tabs may become better multitaskers, but this can fragment their focus. Anecdotally, I deal with this daily as an adult. I couldn't imagine getting anything done as a teenager with this much access.

Altered Brain Development

Most of the literature aimed at new parents zooms in on the fact that birth to age 5 is one of the most critical periods of development in their lives. It's why we hover like helicopters making sure we do the right thing as much as possible to set them up for success. For some of us, it might be jarring to hear that research shows that excessive screen use can affect the development of neural pathways, especially in younger children. According to John S. Hutton and team in their piece "Home Reading Environment and Brain Activation in Preschool Children Listening to Stories," preschool children who listened to stories showed activation of "brain areas supporting mental imagery and narrative comprehension."[8] Note: this had nothing to do with an iPad or YouTube—two tools we all have probably used too much with our children in early childhood. In a 2023 *Cureus Journal of Medical Science* piece full of powerful data (seriously, if you are digging this chapter I'd read the whole publication) it states that "Early screen exposure has been associated with lower cognitive abilities and academic performance in later years."[9]

The growing human brain is constantly building neural connections while pruning away less-used ones, and digital media use plays an active role in that process, according to Pediatrician Michael Rich, director of the Center on Media and Child Health at Boston Children's Hospital, associate professor of pediatrics at HMS, and associate professor of social and behavioral sciences at the Harvard T.H. Chan School of Public Health.[10]

When your children are old enough to read, read some of these studies to them. Learn with them instead of lecture at them. They are curious creatures just like us.

Overstimulation

It shouldn't take more than five minutes of watching content marketed to children or a degree in rocket science to gather that the fast-paced, colorful content on screens can overstimulate the brain, leading to difficulties in calming down or transitioning to slower activities.[11] Ask any parent who has ever tried to tell their child to step away from a screen. There is no joy in that situation, for parent or child. Increased sensitivity to digital rewards leads to dissatisfaction in and desensitization of the real world. Additionally, multitasking and rapid task-switching, common with technology use, can overload a child's brain, making it harder to process information effectively.

When examining the physiology of the brain, it's important to note that "Human cognitive architecture and brain functioning only allows for switching between different tasks (i.e., performing a number of different tasks or partial tasks in quick succession) rather than the simultaneous performance of tasks, even though the performance seems subjectively to occur simultaneously."[12]

Decreased Impulse Control

According to a 2017 piece in *Frontiers in Psychology*, the "instant rewards" in apps and games can make it harder for children to develop self-control and delay gratification. This piece goes on to state that "there is a common belief that the current generation of children and teenagers are less capable of waiting for rewards, due in part to the omnipresence of various types of multimedia in their lives."[13] Video games and social media's reward systems (likes, points, notifications, sounds) can heighten a child's sensitivity to immediate rewards, affecting decision-making and impulse control.[14] We have a new generation of children that essentially can't deal with boredom like generations prior, have little to no patience, and have a decreased ability to creatively problem-solve in the moment.[15]

Improved Hand–Eye Coordination

Let's get positive for a moment: using devices like video games can improve hand–eye coordination, as players often need to react quickly and precisely. Now does that mean your three-year-old should be spending hours playing *Roblox* or *Call of Duty*? Nope. But according to *Psychological Science*, "Playing action video games enhances several different aspects of visual processing."[16]

Weaker Social Cognition

Heavy screen use, especially on social media, can reduce children's ability to read social cues and understand facial expressions. According to Yalda T. Uhls, "Skills in reading human emotion may be diminished when children's face-to-face interaction is displaced by technologically mediated communication."[17] In a world where we are more connected yet lonelier than ever, I can't think of a more pressing skillset we should focus on—especially with our youth. Social cues are important nuances that are easily lost in text-based communications. Let's not let our children's social skills be reduced to mastering the perfect caption on an Instagram post or a snarky comment on a TikTok. Interpersonal connection will beat quick edits and fast cuts any day—and the common media landscape of social media is best saved for after those critical skills are developed (and dare I say, mastered). Additionally, we are seeing altered language development in younger children given that verbal interactions with caregivers have been replaced with child and adult faces in screens. This perpetuates the cycle of these weakened face-to-face skills.

Enhanced Learning

Here's another positive amid some pretty staggering negatives. Educational tools, games, and apps *can* support learning by making abstract concepts more tangible and interactive. I place emphasis on the "can" as this requires adequate filters, time limits, and restrictions so that curious minds don't veer off course and onto ChatGPT. According to Richard E. Mayer, "People can learn more deeply from words and pictures than from words alone."[18] He should know, as the Distinguished Professor of Psychology at University of California, Santa Barbara, and the author of more than 500 publications.

Altered Dopamine System

A quick Google search for "effects of screens on dopamine" netted the following result:

> Screen time can affect dopamine in the brain in several ways:
>
> - **Dopamine Release:** Screen time, like using social media or playing video games, can trigger dopamine release, which is often associated with pleasure.
> - **Desensitization:** Prolonged exposure to dopamine from screen time can desensitize the brain's reward system. This means that the brain needs more dopamine to feel the same amount of pleasure, and it may become harder to stop using screens.
> - **Dopamine-driven Habits:** Screen time can influence habits, such as how people spend their time, their diet, and their mental health.
> - **Negative Effects on Impulse Control:** Screen time can negatively affect impulse control.

- **Dopamine Spikes in Children:** Screen time can trigger dopamine surges in children, which can lead to them wanting to continue the activities.
- **Sleep Disruption:** Using screens at night can disrupt sleep, which is important for children.

With multiple sources contributing to the previous bullet points.

One source that helped to shape these results, titled "Anti-dopamine parenting' can curb a kid's craving for screens or sweets," has so many gems that honestly you should read the whole thing—but two quotes that really stood out to me:

- "Turns out, smartphones and sugary foods do have something in common with drugs: they trigger surges of a neurotransmitter deep inside your brain called dopamine. Although drugs cause much bigger spikes of dopamine than, say, social media or an ice cream cone, these smaller spikes still influence our behavior, especially in the long run. They shape our habits, our diets, our mental health and how we spend our free time. They can also cause much conflict between parents and children."
- "So I tell parents, 'It's not you versus your child, but rather it's you versus a hijacked neural pathway. It's the dopamine you're fighting. And that's not a fair fight,'" says Emily Cherkin, who spent more than a decade teaching middle school and now coaches parents about screens.[19]

What else do we need to hear to be convinced that these screens have a major impact on our brains? And from whom? I know I'm pretty clear now on where I went wrong with screens and my only son. I truly wish I could go back in time and make drastic changes, and I hope you have that opportunity ahead of you.

Getting Our Fix

I'll come right out and say it: we are a society addicted to screens. It is no different than any other addiction. If you look at alcohol use disorders, there's a direct correlation between the age of the first drink and the probability of going on to develop addiction. So a young brain is much more susceptible to some of these habits and the reward system that follows. And, of course, the neuroscientists working with the largest technology companies know all of this. Just ask Dr. Marci!

I found an article recently on the Living Skills in the Schools website that speaks to the addiction directly, without mincing words, around what happens with dopamine dependency and technology:

> What these students are experiencing is the chemical process of tolerance, dependence, and addiction. Addiction is based on dopamine dependence. Dopamine is the brain's chemical signal for pleasure, excitement, and motivation. The addiction process begins through the hacking of the dopamine system by an outside source. The dopamine becomes spiked, dysregulated, and the brain is flooded with this chemical.
>
> This may sound like a pleasurable process; and for a brief moment, it is. The issues begin the moment the outside source is removed, and the dopamine dips below normal levels. A phase of discomfort and discontentment ensues, leaving the individual clamoring for the most immediate source of dopamine. Only through a sustained period of abstinence from this outside source does the brain return to normal levels, and the individual is returned to their original equilibrium.[20]

Screen Addiction, Children's Withdrawal Behavior, and the Parental Role

Coming off screens can be so telling. Sometimes, for hours they spend immersed in a completely different world, connecting with what's within the game and perhaps other people playing the game as well. These connections are all virtual connections. Once off screens, for whatever reason a parent pulls them off, then they're ripped back into this reality. Everything they've been living has been erased—even if only momentarily. And their reaction is so visceral, so real.

Once these little ones are ripped off screens to go to school or to soccer practice or to the store—basically anything that disrupts their online session—the struggle is real. For most, it's not easy. At best, they simply whine and dig their heels in. But at worst, it's an entirely different, other-worldly reaction—maybe something more reminiscent of *The Exorcist*. Maybe they get so mad that they fly into a blind rage. Maybe they immediately demand a snack or a meal. Maybe they get off kindly and nicely and go about what's next. But I doubt it. It's been my experience, and that of others too, from hearing so many other stories, that it's an absolute nightmare. But why is this?

For one, these children have been activating the pleasure center of their brains in a completely different world for hours. So it makes sense that their reaction would be similar to an addict detoxing. If they're ripped out of that world and then are forced to exist in the real world with real demands, responsibilities, feelings, and people, it's certainly going to be an adjustment to find some normalcy and make that transition seamlessly, right? When you take that away without weaning them off, we observe symptoms of withdrawal, including anger and outbursts.

What happens to an addict when they can't get their fix? They resort to extreme behaviors. So it makes sense that this happens when reality yanks your children out of the fantasy land they've been living in for the past six hours. Likely, their friends were there. They haven't had to look around. They've been fully immersed—virtual reality headset or not—in a world with a screen or giant TV, incredible sound systems, and interactive earpieces.

There's Hope: Neuroplasticity and Recovery

This chapter is not meant to cast doom and gloom. In fact, the brain can repair and rewire itself. This powerful idea of neuroplasticity can be conveyed to a child through a metaphor around snow-covered ski slopes.

Per my conversation with Dr. Marci, the brain and neural networks are the ski slopes with well-run paths and tracks. Our thoughts and actions are like the typical skiers that will go down the part of the slope that's been used—the part that has a clear path.

Now, imagine a snowstorm so big it wipes out the whole mountain and now you can ski anywhere you want. That's the ability our brain has to reset out of these dopamine-hijacked routines and addictions. We just need to create the storm.

There's always a chance. There's always hope. But it's time for a reboot.

In the next chapter, we are going to look at how screens affect our bodies, even more so than how we've seen their impact on the brain. Again, don't worry. What we can and should do about all of this is coming. Sit tight and keep reading.

Notes

1. *Personal conversation with Dr. Marci, 9:52 minute mark, May 2024.*

2. Ferguson, C.J. and Donnellan, M.B. (2014). Is the association between children's baby video viewing and poor language development robust? A reanalysis of Zimmerman, Christakis, and Meltzoff (2007). *Developmental Psychology*. https://pubmed.ncbi.nlm.nih.gov/23855259/.

3. Danielson, M.L. et al. (2022). *Journal of Clinical Child & Adolescent Psychology*. https://www.tandfonline.com/doi/full/10.1080/15374416.2024.2335625#abstract.

4. Christakis, D.A. (2009). The effects of fast-paced cartoons. *Pediatrics*. https://doi.org/10.1542/peds.2011-2071.

5. Sparrow, B., Liu, J., and Wegner, D.M. (2011). Google effects on memory: cognitive consequences of having information at our fingertips. *Science*. https://www.science.org/doi/10.1126/science.1207745.

6. Prensky, M. (2001). Digital game-based learning. *Computers in Entertainment (CIE)*. https://dl.acm.org/doi/10.1145/950566.950596.

7. Ophir, E., Nass, C., and Wagner, A.D. (2009). *Proceedings of the National Academy of Sciences of the United States of America*. https://pubmed.ncbi.nlm.nih.gov/19706386/.

8. Hutton, J.S. et al. (2015). Home reading environment and brain activation in preschool children listening to stories. *Pediatrics*. https://pubmed.ncbi.nlm.nih.gov/26260716/.

9. Muppalla, S.K., et al. (2023). Effects of excessive screen time on child development: an updated review and strategies for management. https://www.ncbi.nlm.nih.gov/pmc/articles/PMC10353947/#:~:text=The%20Quebec%20Longitudinal%20Study%20of,mathematics%20and%20English%20%5B9%5D.

10. Ruder, D.R. (2019). Screen time and the brain. *Harvard Medical School*. https://hms.harvard.edu/news/screen-time-brain.

11. Christakis, D.A. (2014). Interactive media use at younger than the age of 2 years: time to rethink the American Academy of Pediatrics guideline? *JAMA Pediatrics*. 168 (5): 399–400. 10.1001/jamapediatrics.2013.5081.

12. Kirschner, P.A. and van Merrinboer, J.J.G. (2013). Do learners really know best? *Urban Legends in Education, Educational Psychologist* 48 (3): 169–183. https://doi.org/10.1080/00461520.2013.804395.

13. Wilmer, H.H., Sherman, L.E., and Chein, J.M. (2017). Smartphones and cognition: a review of research exploring the links between mobile technology habits and cognitive functioning. *Frontiers in Psychology.* https://www.frontiersin.org/journals/psychology/articles/10.3389/fpsyg.2017.00605/full.

14. Lérida-Ayala, V. et al. (2023). Internet and video games: causes of behavioral disorders in children and teenagers. *Children (Basel).* https://www.ncbi.nlm.nih.gov/pmc/articles/PMC9856521/.

15. Deng, X. et al. (2021). Differences in reward sensitivity between high and low problematic smartphone use adolescents: an ERP study. *International Journal of Environmental Research and Public Health.* https://www.ncbi.nlm.nih.gov/pmc/articles/PMC8470587/.

16. Green, C.S. and Bavelier, D. (2007). Action-video-game experience alters the spatial resolution of vision. *Psychological Science.* https://www.ncbi.nlm.nih.gov/pmc/articles/PMC2896830/.

17. Uhls, Y.T. et al. (2014). Five days at outdoor education camp without screens improves preteens' ability to read nonverbal emotion cues. *Computers in Human Behavior.* https://www.sciencedirect.com/science/article/pii/S0747563214003227.

18. Mayer, R.E. (2014). Introduction to multimedia learning. In: *The Cambridge Handbook of Multimedia Learning*, 2e (ed. R.E. Mayer), 1–24. Cambridge University Press. https://psycnet.apa.org/record/2015-00153-001.

19. Doucleff, M. (2023). 'Anti-dopamine parenting' can curb a kid's craving for screens or sweets. *NPR.* https://www.npr.org/sections/health-shots/2023/06/12/1180867083/tips-to-outsmart-dopamine-unhook-kids-from-screens-sweets#:~:text=Turns%20out%2C%20smartphones%20and%20sugary,conflict%20between%20parents%20and%20children.

20. Danny, Z. (2023). Growing up and growing risks. *Living Skills in Schools.* https://livingskillsintheschools.org/uncategorized/growing-up-and-growing-risks/?gad_source=1&gclid=CjwKCAjw3NyxBhBmEiwAyofDYS_yC9a6RHPM7jbyCDf7MpCVOzefNfgrPFFxsd12BHnlo-Wb8ozpXhoCqjsQAvD_BwE.

6 | Digital Effects on the Body

"Technology can feel like a lifeline. It can feel like an umbilical cord and let's think about what happens when those are cut: we are launched into the real world and have to learn to breathe and eat on our own. When technological connection feels like an umbilical cord connection, technology can create nervous system responses that are designed for life-threatening situations."

—*Dee Wagner*[1]

Besides the dance of relationship between caregiver and child, one of the big a-has I gathered from speaking with Dee Wagner was understanding the importance of movement, or embodiment.

"My understanding of trauma is simply inhibited movement in the body," she said.

She went on to recall stories of folks so out of touch with their bodies that they could not receive the message from their nervous system. Those signals of stimulation or satiation, or stimulation overload, and mindless Internet surfing exemplify shutdown as opposed to going for a walk or engaging in a hobby.

Polyvagal theory explains that our bodies have different biological responses when we feel safe enough for social engagement. When we are using the biology that is designed for social engagement, we are present in our bodies and can feel sensory satiation. We can even pay attention to the messages coming from our bodies to our brains.

In this chapter, let's take a look at what happens to our bodies as related to sitting or lying down or going across our day (and night) glued to a screen.

Children's Bodies Overall

Physiologically, our children's bodies are maturing faster than ever before. As for the reason, no one can nail it down for certain. Some cite diet, obesity, genetics, socioeconomic status, or chemical exposure.

What we do know is that for girls from ages 8 to 13 the average age of puberty's onset in America has been lowered by around three months each decade over the past 40 years.[2] But here's the scary part: while their bodies are maturing earlier and earlier, we are learning that their brains don't fully mature until well into their twenties.[3] Specifically, we are talking particularly about the prefrontal cortex (which we discussed in more detail in the last chapter)—the place in the brain where decisions are made.

Our children are walking around with adult bodies, undeveloped brains, and unlimited access to everything in the known universe in the back pocket of their jeans.[4] I mean, what could go wrong?

Sitting Is the New Smoking

There's a reason we want to move when we're watching people move on a screen. Wagner explained to me how mirror neurons pattern our brain as we have moved.[5] Have you ever wondered why instructional videos for martial artists exist? Or football players watch films to prepare for a pending opponent? Humans watch videos to pattern their brains around movement thanks to our mirror neurons.

But no one on the planet can simply master any move *simply by watching*. They have to get moving themselves. They have to try it. Watching is just the beginning of an awakening movement. As Wagner explains:

> If we move together or dance together, then all of that that got stirred up in you when you had your screen time is getting met, then you are more likely to grow tired of just watching and so your mirror neurons just say, hey I'm tired of screens. I'm tired of watching now.[6]

It's like the athletes who watch the screens say, okay I'd like to try it now. Ultimately, we learn to recognize our own need to move. But these athletes are highly incentivized to move or they are adults who realize how important it is for them to physically perform what they see on the screen.

Now, let's look at our children's bodies. Say they eat three wholesome, well-balanced meals yet spend their time seated on a couch or a beanbag or on the floor staring at a screen. For hours. Are they getting outside and moving to burn anything? Not as much as they used to. What do you think is happening to all that energy provided by their food? Hint: It's nothing.

Just like an athlete needs to stop watching and get moving to perfect their skills, children need to stop watching and get moving to stay healthy.

The body requires a certain number of calories to operate on the basic level, fueling involuntary movements like blinking or heartbeats and normal functioning of our muscular systems and organs. It's letting their young bodies operate, but they are certainly not burning enough calories to compensate for being sedentary. The calories add up and the conversion to fat stores increases, and obesity can set in. In fact, the risk of childhood obesity increases dramatically when young people aren't moving, and the sedentary lifestyle that embraces gaming or video consumption is a contributing factor.

While every human body is different and children's metabolisms are much faster than adults, sitting around for hours certainly doesn't help the fight against childhood obesity. If they're sitting, they are not moving, and nothing is more simple to comprehend than that.

Our bodies, adult and child alike, are not meant to be sedentary for hours upon hours each day. We were made to move. And between eight hours a day of school, mostly sitting, and then multiple hours in the evening at home—again, sitting—this does not bode well for the outlook of this generation's health.

If a child or adult is sitting in front of a screen for more than two hours at a time, it's time to take a break. We've got to move our bodies if we are physically able. We've got to let our eyes and our ears focus on something else, get our heart pumping, and just take a break from the gamification and algorithms. Sure we use smart watches to track our every step, but when will we pay attention to what our bodies are telling us here? I mean, the science is already there[7]:

> Numerous factors are associated with childhood obesity including increased dietary intake of high-fat snacks and fast foods, large portion sizes, increased consumption of sugar sweetened beverages and other environmental and genetic factors; however, lack of regular physical activity and sedentary lifestyle is one of the most important determinant of childhood obesity.

Humans were never meant to sit for long periods of time, and if they can take a break every couple of hours to move their bodies and use their other senses, they will be healthier and happier for it (physically and mentally).

Sitting around watching traditional TV, with television commercials, also has some less obvious effects. One, it exposes you to food advertising, which as you know works. People exposed to food advertising literally grab more snacks and foods, right? Advertising works. We know that. Nielsen knows that. It's worked for decades and decades, and it will continue to work. So, food advertising is one thing.

But then the second thing is that the media—traditional and social—distracts us from what's called satiety, the feeling of being full. We're too busy watching the show or scrolling a feed to realize that actually *we're full and that we should stop eating*. Or we're so hypnotized that we forget that we were ever hungry or thirsty before we started playing the video game or consuming the content. We see this when our show ends or our game is over and we head straight for the kitchen for a feast.

There's another problem that presents itself here as well. Screen-induced inactivity can tend lead to us making poor, or less healthy, food choices, especially when we are too "busy" to prepare wholesome food choices. Most "snacks" today are created to not only be quick but also saltier or more flavorful. There are more on the unhealthy side than the healthy side, as it's so much faster/easier to grab a bag of potato chips rather than clean off some carrots.

According to Edward R. Laskowski, M.D., "Research has linked sitting for long periods of time with a number of health concerns. They include obesity and a cluster of conditions — increased blood pressure, high blood sugar, excess body fat around the waist and unhealthy cholesterol levels — that make up metabolic syndrome. Too much sitting overall and prolonged periods of sitting also seem to increase the risk of death from cardiovascular disease and cancer."[8]

The bottom line is that, as parents, we need to monitor our children's screen time to be sure they are getting enough physical activity to keep them healthy.

Competition and Comparison

When I was growing up, I would see the glorified models inside a *Cosmopolitan*, *Vogue*, or some other type of fashion magazine that definitely did not look like me. They had bodies that did not look like mine. They wore clothes that I will never be able to afford. But I could at least put that magazine away and not be faced with it until the next one came out the next month.

Today, kids have this exposure in their pockets any time they want it. Models and influencers have filtered faces, perfectly sculpted bodies, six-pack abs, super straight and white teeth, no acne or wrinkles whatsoever, and big full lips. And it's just, it's crazy. It's absolute madness. Some of the non-AI-generated humans you seen online today don't even look like real humans—yet *they* are now the standard for beauty. They are now the barometer that our children are using to measure their external self-worth.

Children want to be like them, and they have easy access to information about how to restrict calories or which beauty products will give them the fixes they most deeply desire for things that don't need to be fixed. Year over year at Bark, our annual report has shown that disordered eating is the one statistic that has consistently gotten worse—and it's not just with adolescent girls but with boys too.

Speaking of disordered eating, have you heard about the Internet hashtag #Thinspo? Thinspo is a deviation of the popular hashtag #inspo, which is an abbreviated form of "inspiration." So #thinspo is the Instagram hashtag for "thin inspiration."

For many years without oversight and with hundreds of thousands of followers, this hashtag (think of it as a television channel where post content is aggregated) showcased various, mostly female midriffs of teens, tweens, and young adult women. Pelvic bones, collar bones, exposed ribs, and extremely thin bodies are showcased here for people to draw on for their thin inspiration or their thinspo.

Thankfully, Meta has taken steps to address this specific hashtag, but new ones pop up daily across a variety of platforms. An Instagram search for #thinspo today takes you to a page featuring the header "Help is Available" with text immediately below it that states "If you or someone you know may be struggling, there are ways to get help." It then features the contact info for a helpline, the ability to reach a friend, and suggestions from professionals outside of Meta to get help. This is encouraging, but more needs to be done. In fact, according to Fairplay, a nonprofit based in Boston, Massachusetts, that is "committed to helping children thrive in an increasingly commercialized, screen-obsessed culture," Meta actually "profits from pushing pro-eating disorder content to children on Instagram."[9]

Whether it's Meta (Instagram), YouTube, TikTok, or the next popular platform, we can be sure of one thing: this "Look at me, pay attention to me" culture is only going to perpetuate more comparison traps that harm those most vulnerable: children with low self-esteem.

Eyes On, Lights Out

Right now, there are many studies investigating the effect of blue light on the body. And what is blue light? Good question. I'll break it down the best I know how. Most light in the natural world contains blue light. In fact, according to UC Davis, "About one-third of all visible light is considered blue light," and that big glowing ball of fire in the sky, the sun, produces the most blue light. Blue light has the shortest wavelengths but packs a punch with the highest energy.[10]

If you're interested in the details, the bulk of this light coming from smartphones, TVs, and tablets have wavelengths between 400 and 490 nanometers. That's key, because when we're gazing into Mario's world, all that light in a darkened room is pouring directly into the eye and then the optic nerve and then is processed in the brain.

But it doesn't take any studies to know that the light from our screens isn't the healthiest for our eyes. In fact, nearly 7 out of 10 Americans claim to suffer eye strain, blurred vision, dry or irritated eyes, headaches, and even migraines from staring at screens for too long.

There's also this to consider when having bright screen light inches from our face well past sundown. What does the brain think if it's getting a late-night dose of near sunlight? Well, it thinks it's daylight, of course. And not only is the brain literally vibrating with this energy, but melatonin levels drop.

Melatonin is a hormone the brain releases, mostly, in darkness as an aid to slow our circadian rhythms and allow for sleep, rest, and repair. Basically, the more and longer we're scrolling, the longer our body will take to slow down to sleep—after we shut down our device.[11]

At the same time, there are emerging studies that claim the concerns over blue light may be a bit exaggerated. A recent study by researchers at the University of Basel in Switzerland concludes that blue light may not, in fact, be the primary factor in affecting our "internal clock."

The scientists affirmed the long-standing evidence that the sleep/wake cycle is controlled by Ganglion cells in the eye. Yet other photoreceptors (you may know them as the cones—as in rods and cones) encode the color of light itself and could play a factor.

"Our results support the findings of many other studies that the light-sensitive ganglion cells are most important for the human internal clock," Dr. Christine Blume, a psychologist at the Centre for Chronobiology of the University of Basel in Switzerland, explained.

The shift in brightness and light color like from orange to blueish, or vice versa, occurs around dusk and dawn, and has long signaled nightfall or the birth of the coming day. You might hear crickets, cicadas and owls, or a rooster and or tons of other morning birds to understand this part.

"The problem is that in everyday language we often refer to the short-wavelength light to which the specialized ganglion cells are most sensitive as 'blue light,'" she said. "This is despite the fact that the light does not have to be perceived as blue."

"Therefore, short-wavelength light—misleadingly often termed 'blue light'—should be reduced in the evening, for example by dimming computer screens and using a night-shift mode. Avoiding screen time before bed can also help, as the things we do on our phones often delay sleep."[12]

However, one thing is clear. If your child is on a screen, playing a video game, doing their homework in bed on a computer, or just good ol' fashioned reading by lamplight, they aren't sleeping. And almost every organization who studies this issue firmly suggests that all screens should be removed from their bedrooms at least 30–60 minutes before bedtime. And I don't need to tell you the importance of sleep for all people, not just our offspring who rely on sleep to grow optimally and at a super rapid pace.

During the teenage years, sleep is critical. Yet around the same time our children need more sleep than ever, they are given devices that keep them up. As responsible parents and caregivers, we have to get screens out of the room, smartphones, gaming consoles, school-issued devices, and televisions OUT. OF. THE. BEDROOMS. We need to turn the Internet off to those respective devices, and essentially shut it all down so our children's brains and bodies can reset. I'll tell you how to do this, by the way, in Chapter 8, "Solutions: So What Do We Do?"

Kids need to sleep. It's the most important thing for their brain and their mental health. End of story.

Sexual Dysfunction

Today there is a growing epidemic in young teenage boys of erectile dysfunction. Why do you think that is? It's because exposure to sexually suggestive or downright explicit material happens earlier than ever.

For many Boomers and Gen Xers, their experience seeing a naked person was likely a *National Geographic* picture exposé, or an old *Playboy* magazine. Today, boys, teens, and young men (women too) are watching Internet porn in high definition downloaded over high-speed connections. The majority of time, they're alone, so masturbation is also likely.

When they're mature and developing a relationship where they can share their early sexual experiences with a consensual partner, performance suddenly becomes an issue. Once with a living, breathing partner, they can't get an erection. They're too distracted. They're overwhelmed. They're freaked out. They're not in their routine. There is no functional issue, vascularly or muscularly.

But we're seeing erectile dysfunction levels at the same level as older men. We're hearing about situations where young men must refrain from watching any sort of sexually explicit material, be it pornography or other imagery, for a year or two to reboot and to get back on track. Some also find a link between the prevalence of online pornography and violence toward women in general. If you look at the numbers around sexual aggression, those rates have gone up significantly over the years, and exposure to pornography at a young age is one possible factor.

According to Fight The New Drug (FTND), a highly respected, "non-religious and non-legislative nonprofit that exists to provide individuals the opportunity to make an informed decision regarding pornography by raising awareness on its harmful effects using only science, facts, and personal accounts,"[13] pornography harms us (collectively) in three ways: as individuals, in relationships, and as a society. In fact, if you visit https://truthaboutporn .org, you will see an updated and growing database of research to support these findings.

While the previous chapter covered how technology impacts our brains and this chapter delves more into how tech affects our bodies, pornography impacts both. Again, according to FTND, "Like it or not, porn consumption entails pleasure, focus, and repetition. These factors create the perfect conditions for Delta-FosB build-up and the formation of long-lasting pathways in the brain. It can also provide an overabundance of supernormal stimuli that can completely rewire what we find arousing and what we desire and expect from sexual intimacy. These changes in our expectations can have tremendous implications for how we view others and how we view relationships."[14]

Our children are encountering this content without our knowledge or consent, across devices we buy them and that school systems instruct them to use, and it's negatively impacting their ability to have healthy, consensual, sexual relationships once they are old enough and mature enough to do so.

Dr. Google

Before the Internet, if you were ill, you had to rely on a wise parent, experienced grandparent, pediatrician, primary-care physician, or specialist to tell you what your symptoms likely indicated about your health and well-being. Now, medical advice is a Dr. Google search away or, worse, a TikTok search fraught with misinformation.

In fact, on a recent comedy special, a comedian was joking about how entering a few symptoms into WedMD rarely gives you just one result and it's so true! Your sniffles and persistent cough could be just a little baby cold or seven other things, including lung cancer. Turning to the Internet as an adult to self-diagnose is scary enough. Now imagine being a child and thinking your headache is a brain tumor when really you are just dehydrated and need more rest.

This issue becomes even more problematic when a child starts looking up ways to lose weight, or restrict calories, or tries to self-diagnose a perceived mental health issue—not to mention the millions of other reasons why someone might seek medical information on the Internet in order to not see a professional.

Just a Few More

In addition to lack of movement, obesity, disordered eating, eye strain, sleep disturbances, stunted growth, sexual dysfunction, and misdiagnosis of symptoms—here are a few other impacts of tech on our bodies to close out this chapter (yes, there are more, and there's actually a positive one listed):

- Poor posture (slouching for extended periods of time negatively impacts the neck, back, and shoulders)[15]
- Fine motor skill development (this one is actually a positive as children are spending less time using writing utensils, but please note the answer isn't to hand them a PS5 controller instead of a pencil)[16]
- Reduced physical strength (outside of muscles surrounding your scrolling thumbs, more time spent on screens equals less time spent on activities that build muscle strength and endurance)[17]
- Increased risk of repetitive strain injuries (this is the con to the pro mentioned two bullet points ago as frequent use of handheld devices can lead to very specific injuries in the wrists, hands, and fingers)[18]
- Delayed motor skills development (when children spend less time moving their bodies in big ways—running, jumping, etc.—it can slow down the development of their gross motor skills)[19]
- Weaker immune system (from lack of physical activity)[20]

So, the next time your child asks why they need a screen break, feel free to refer to this chapter to help them understand the way technology impacts their body, the chapter before this one to explain brain-specific impacts, and the next chapter on how screen can impact their mind and spirit. Education is power. You now have the power.

Notes

1. Wagner, D. (2016). How polyvagal theory helps me overcome technological disembodiment. *Elephant Journal.* https://www.elephant journal.com/2016/09/overcoming-technologys-potential-to-disembody-how-polyvagal-theory-helps-me-picture-it/.

2. Hopkins, C. (2023). With puberty starting earlier than ever, doctors urge greater awareness and care. *NBC News.* https://www.nbcnews.com/health/kids-health/puberty-starting-earlier-treatment-children-rcna125441.

3. National Institute of Mental Health (n.d.). The teen brain: 7 things to know. https://www.nimh.nih.gov/health/publications/the-teen-brain-7-things-to-know#:~:text=Although%20the%20brain%20stops%20growing,the%20last%20parts%20to%20mature.

4. Eckert-Lind, C. et al. (2020). Worldwide secular trends in age at pubertal onset assessed by breast development among girls. *JAMA Pediatrics.* https://www.ncbi.nlm.nih.gov/pmc/articles/PMC7042934/.

5. Kilner, J.M. and Lemon, R.N. (2013). What we know currently about mirror neurons. *Current Biology.* https://www.ncbi.nlm.nih.gov/pmc/articles/PMC3898692/.

6. *Personal conversation with Dee Wagner.*

7. Ramírez-Coronel, A.A., Abdu, W.J., Alshahrani, S.H. et al. (2023). RETRACTED ARTICLE: Childhood obesity risk increases with increased screen time: a systematic review and dose–response meta-analysis. *Journal of Health, Population and Nutrition* 42: 5. https://jhpn.biomedcentral.com/articles/10.1186/s41043-022-00344-4#:~:text=The%20obesity%2Dpromoting%20effects%20of%20increased%20screen%2Dtime%20can%20be,children%20and%20adolescents%20%5B82%2C83.

8. Laskowski, E.R. (n.d.). What are the risks of sitting too much? *Mayo Clinic.* https://www.mayoclinic.org/healthy-lifestyle/adult-health/expert-answers/sitting/faq-20058005.

9. Monahan, D. (2022). April 14, 2022. New report shows Meta profits from pushing pro-eating disorder content to children on Instagram. *Fairplay for Kids.* https://fairplayforkids.org/april-14-2022-new-meta-profits-from-pushing-pro-eating-disorder-content-to-children-on-instagram/.

10. Barnett, M. (2022). How blue light affects your eyes, sleep, and health. *U. C. Davis Health*. https://health.ucdavis.edu/blog/cultivating-health/blue-light-effects-on-your-eyes-sleep-and-health/2022/08#:~:text=Blue%20light%20is%20part%20of,biggest%20source%20of%20blue%20light.

11. Shoemaker, S. (2023). How screens affect your Sleep—it goes beyond blue light. *Forbes*. https://www.forbes.com/sites/forbes-personal-shopper/article/how-screens-affect-sleep/?sh=4ce1c4ac28a8.

12. Pelc, C. (2024). Blue light may not affect your sleep-wake cycle, study finds. *Medical News Today*. https://www.medicalnewstoday.com/articles/blue-light-may-not-affect-sleep-wake-cycle.

13. Fight the New Drug website. https://fightthenewdrug.org/about/.

14. Fight the New Drug (n.d.). How porn can change the brain. https://fightthenewdrug.org/how-porn-can-change-the-brain/.

15. Straker, L. and Mathiassen, S.E. (2009). Increased physical workloads in modern work – a necessity for better health and performance? *Ergonomics*. https://pubmed.ncbi.nlm.nih.gov/19787501/.

16. Grissom, J.B. (2005). Physical fitness and academic achievement. *Journal of Exercise Physiology*. https://citeseerx.ist.psu.edu/document?repid=rep1&type=pdf&doi=aeca4da5eaced49b823b871a5a0081d806010908.

17. Tremblay, M.S. et al. (2011). Systematic review of sedentary behaviour and health indicators in school-aged children and youth. *International Journal of Behavioral Nutrition and Physical Activity*. https://ijbnpa.biomedcentral.com/articles/10.1186/1479-5868-8-98.

18. OrthoVirginia (n.d.). The virtual athlete: the rise of video gaming and related injuries. https://www.orthovirginia.com/blog/the-virtual-athlete-the-rise-of-video-gaming-and/.

19. Carson, V. et al. (2016). Systematic review of physical activity and cognitive development in early childhood. *Journal of Science and Medicine in Sport*. https://pubmed.ncbi.nlm.nih.gov/26197943/.

20. Gleeson, M. et al. (2011). The immune response to exercise: role of neuroendocrine and metabolic responses. *Immunology and Cell Biology*. https://pubmed.ncbi.nlm.nih.gov/17303714/.

7

Digital Effects on Mind/Spirit

People don't get depressed when they face threats collectively;
they get depressed when they feel isolated, lonely, or useless.
—*Jonathan Haidt*, The Anxious Generation

This chapter explores the complex relationship between digital connectivity and its impact on our mental and emotional well-being. It delves into the paradox of how, despite being more connected than ever through digital means, many people feel increasingly isolated and disconnected on a deeper, emotional level. The chapter discusses the influence of screen culture on family dynamics, child development, and the nervous system, highlighting the potential consequences of overreliance on digital devices. It also examines the effects of media violence and social media–induced anxiety, such as fear of missing out (FOMO), while offering insights into how mindful use of technology can mitigate these negative effects.

This chapter will give you a deeper understanding of the subtle yet profound ways digital technology is shaping our minds, spirits, and relationships. Whether you're a parent concerned about your child's development, an individual struggling with the pressures of social media, or simply someone interested in the broader impact of technology on society, this chapter has something for you. After reading this (and in conjunction with Chapter 8, "Solutions: So What Do We Do?"), you will have practical advice on how to navigate the digital world more consciously, fostering healthier mental and emotional well-being for yourself and those around you.

The Great Disconnect

Never before have we been so "connected" as a society yet so entirely disconnected and lonely inside. Look around the room the next time you are in a group of humans. You may see people together in close physical proximity, but are they truly together? Are they talking to each other face to face, or are their faces buried in smartphones?

So many parents are sitting within an arm's length from their child and they're both on their phones or on a digital device that's connected somehow to the Internet. And the mom, for example (dad too), might be scrolling on Instagram looking at everybody's best and brightest lives. Meanwhile, their child is potentially consuming harmful content or communicating with dangerous people, unbeknownst to their parent. Keep in mind, this is happening within the walls of the home that we work so hard to protect—with locks on the doors and fresh batteries in the smoke detectors.

Psychiatrists and mental health therapists specializing in attachment and nervous system science, like Dr. Marci, Dee Wagner, or Caroline Gebhardt (all of whom you were introduced to earlier in this book), have all pointed to the value of human relationships, particularly the parent-to-child relationship that has the most potential for nervous system patterning and relational imprints.

"When young people of all ages are handed a screen for soothing more relational and developmental needs rather than using screens for limited entertainment or intentional education purposes, I see more dis-ease and dis-embodiment," Gebhardt said.

This means the less someone can explore the world through hands-on, physical experiences, the less likely they are to be capable of engaging in physical activity, leading to the sort of health problems discussed in Chapter 6.

As a society, we have created a screen culture—where there is a virtual portal of escape and/or freeze. We've let gaming or television or movies or social media become a chronic coping habit or pastime, inhibiting the physiological functioning one needs for development and social engagement system functioning, as Dr. Stephen Porges pointed out.

According to the National Institute for the Clinical Application of Behavioral Medicine,

> "Dr. Stephen Porges' social engagement system is a network of neural pathways that control the muscles of the face, head, heart, and lungs. It's a key part of Porges' polyvagal theory, which describes how the nervous system responds to safety and threat."[1]

Essentially, the social engagement system is "the first circuit of the nervous system, and a unique mammalian pathway. It's used to send facial expressions and bodily cues to other mammals to indicate if we're safe to approach."[2]

What does this mean in the simplest terms?

It means that critical emotional cues start early and can be delayed if both parent and child have screens in their faces instead of experiencing a decent amount of face-to-face time.

If our children—as babies and toddlers—fall, for example, and look up to gauge a parent or caregiver's reaction and there is none because the adult missed it (because they were immersed in a TikTok or YouTube video), then that child does not learn the proper way to respond empathetically to that event.

What's My Purpose?

Erik Erikson, the popular child psychoanalyst who outlined eight stages of psychosocial development over the course of infancy through adulthood, identified a critical period during adolescence (12–18 years of age) that I'd like to highlight now.

According to Erikson, during this stage tweens and teens encounter the basic conflict of identity versus confusion. They "experiment with and develop identity and roles."[3]

Essentially, two of the most important questions when you're a teenager are:

Who am I?
and
How do I fit in?

So if you give developing young adults unprecedented access, feeds full of filtered faces and bodies, and powerful algorithms that take them places they shouldn't be, you are negatively impacting their sense of self during a critical phase of development.

It's not something that 99.99% of parents intend to do—shift their children's comparison radar into overdrive without the proper tools and conversations—but we are all complicit.

Adolescents aren't properly and physiologically equipped to be connected to the entire Internet, data-grabbing and addictive apps, and more computational power in their pocket than the computers that put man on the moon in 1969. In so many cases this exposure is too much, too fast, and too soon. It would be one thing if they wanted to voraciously read the same amount of content or have the equivalent amount of authentic conversations and in real-life experiences, but that's not happening.

As a result, our children are encountering so many "invisible" (to us) yet traumatic experiences. These experiences are leading to depression, anxiety, loss of sleep, disordered eating, and pornography addictions that can in turn cause them to emotionally and psychologically shut down, or default to "fight-or-flight" mode.

Unless, of course, the parent is two steps ahead—out in front to catch the spiral and validate their child's search for *their* truth. If the parent models the quest to make sense of a world that can seem so senseless, the child can feel the boundary and has the space to find themselves. There's so much confusion in our world already today, and parents need to put up some healthy blinders to limit their children's focus. That creates the desire to keep searching but via a slow roll, if done in a healthy way.

Parental modeling can manifest itself in so many ways—whether it's leaving your own smartphone in a separate place from your body while you connect with other humans, charge it at night in the kitchen instead of bedside, or set time limits for the social media platforms that suck *you* in for too many fleeting moments of your day.

Vocalizing what you, the adult caregiver, experience online goes a long way. Did you see a heated political debate in the Facebook comments section between friends or family members? How did it make you feel? Did it cause you to try a mend a broken bridge? Did it encourage you to fact-check to make sense of what was true and false? Did it make you want to leave the app and never come back? Talk about all of this with your kids. It's part of our new human experience, and they need our adult wisdom to help them navigate these landmines.

The Comparison Trap

Kids often can't distinguish between what they see online and reality. Honestly, adults are often fooled as well. We're all seeing everyone else's staged "highlight reel" and constantly comparing it to our own lives, which then causes us to find our own truly beautiful and blessed lives to be lacking and depressing.

Speaking of a highlight reel, there's also filtered life versus real life. I don't know how many of you watching this have ever experimented with the filters that come with TikTok or Snapchat or Instagram, but there are certain ones that once you put them over your aging adult face, you just don't feel very good about your real self anymore. This can have the same depressing effect on children and teens.

Imagine being a 5th grader or 9th grader going through puberty. Your body is awkward and there's no way around it for the time being. Yet, it seems like nobody else (online) is struggling with clothes that no longer fit well or acne or stretch marks or teeth that could be straighter or whiter or new dimples you've never had before (cellulite). Imagine what that would do to your confidence and sense of self-worth? Unfortunately, we don't have to imagine. It is happening.

Is Nothing Sacred?

Desensitization to violence, including sexual violence, is something that concerns many parents when it comes to their children's tech exposure. It's especially bothersome as more and more children continue to consume more and more media, including violent and overly sexualized video games. While this isn't anything new, the depth and breadth of exposure to this type of content has increased exponentially. Social, political, and scientific debates around the correlation between violence in media and its potential negative effects are now decades long. If you are anywhere near my age, you might remember that whole rating system that emerged in the 80s among the censorship versus family values battles. What you might not know is that content regulation actually started back in 1934 as the Hays Code, a set of guidelines that regulated the content of movies and was created to "restore Hollywood's public image after a series of scandals and to avoid government censorship."[4] This sounds eerily similar to current initiatives, such as Meta launching "Teen Accounts," a purported safer experience for those under 18 on their platform in September 2024, just 24 hours before the Senate Committee Hearing on the Kids Online Safety Act (KOSA).

But things today are on an entirely different level. Parents can no longer trust entities like the Motion Picture Association of America (MPAA) to properly rate and label all of the potential content their children can encounter. There are no PG-13 warnings popping up before each 15-second TikTok video or Instagram reel that a child might consume.

Take the wildly popular gaming series *Grand Theft Auto* (GTA) where players run about the city stealing cars, committing property damage and assaulting and/or killing people graphically. In fact, in GTA 5, soliciting and engaging in sex acts with prostitutes is an actual requirement for completing the game. This game is rated by the Entertainment Software Ratings Board (ESRB) as 18+.

First-person shooter (FPS) games like *Call of Duty* have long been a hot topic in America starting around the time of the first major school shooting (as covered by national media), in Columbine High School on April 20, 1999. Now 25 years, and hundreds of additional and unspeakable multiple-casualty school shootings later, the links between gun violence and violent video games remain a topic of debate.

The term *first-person* describes the perspective the player has while moving around a room, or a battlefield, or a city street. The player looks around as if you're looking through the shooter's eyes—in first-person perspective or point of view. Combined with surround sound and a screen that completely envelopes your peripheral vision, these games are about as fully immersive as you can get.

Then, there's the shooter aspect of it. From ancient guns to modern guns to futuristic guns, these games cover the gamut of projectile-firing arsenal. The details and simulation are exquisite. In some games, players are required to reload clips to continue firing like a real-life situation would entail. Sometimes gun barrels grow too hot. Sometimes guns jam. There are highly accurate scopes and spotting devices. And often upon firing, there are even recoil simulators that shake the physical control violently as the vision of the player in the screen shifts.

The damage of the bullets shifts in terms of accuracy as well. In some games a "hit" will instantly eliminate a target and their body disappears into the ether. In others, only a kill shot will immobilize an enemy and subsequent fire is required until that person is dead. There is blood. There is torn flesh. There are broken bones. There is suffering. Frankly, it's a lot, it's heartbreaking, and it's desensitizing our children to the real cost of violence.

While there's no causal evidence suggesting the connection, most research does suggest that playing violent video games provides an outlet for aggression. "Playing violent games may heighten aggressive behavior, cognition, and affection; increase physiological arousal and hostility; and decrease the probability of helping others (Anderson and Bushman, 2001, 2002; Bushman and Anderson, 2001, 2009; Anderson et al., 2004, 2008; Gentile et al., 2004; Bartholow et al., 2005; Bushman and Huesmann, 2006)."[5]

Just like observing simulated gunshot wounds, horrific head shots, and gruesome deaths portrayed so graphically in the movies, witnessing the same violence depicted in video games also takes a toll on young minds.

Seeing this content time and time again eventually desensitizes us to the horror of it all, and ultimately we grow less empathetic and less disturbed when we see it. The norm should not be getting used to this type of exposure. But studies show players do experience more activated, aggressive feelings brought about by seeing this horror and, in turn, that decreases their empathy and prosocial behavior. In some cases, after people play a violent video game, their brain activation was lower when shown other violent imagery later.

Additionally, how many of you can remember the first graphically violent thing you saw on a screen? For me, two instances stand out.

First, in late elementary school I spent the night out with my friend Mary who happened to have three brothers and whose parents were married and whose dad was a Presbyterian minister. Sounds like a safe place to hang from my parents' perspective, right?

Well, Mary's parents took us all to see a movie that night—in a movie theater, which was very nice of them. Guess what that movie was?

Die Hard: With a Vengeance. The second in the Die Hard series, it was appropriately rated R. Meaning, it was not something that I would have been allowed to see in either of my parents' houses under any circumstances.

The language alone shocked me, but there's a scene (graphic violence warning) where Bruce Willis is fighting a guy outside of a plane and pushes him into the jet engine. After the guy is successfully obliterated—and my 10-year-old eyes saw it all, aghast—he then exclaims a bit later in the movie after blowing up an entire plane, "Yippie kiyay, mother f****er!" I was *floored.*

I think I shot a glance over to Mary's parents to see if they were as shocked as I was, but nope—they were totally engrossed in the movie. Remember, he was a *minister.* It's not that you can't see rated R movies when you are a man of faith or take your kids to those movies as a man of faith, but that's not what I imagined that family was doing on a weekend night. Not in the slightest. My parents would have lost their minds if they knew I was there consuming that content.

I actually just Googled that scene to make sure I had my facts straight (I did) and couldn't even bring myself to watch the full scene. It's still one of the worst things I've ever seen happen to a human, even if it was acting and fake guts.

The next violent scene that I can barely bring myself to think about, much less write about, was unfortunately real and not conceived in a Hollywood studio. I still, to this day, have to actively work to block any memory of a horrific video that a (deranged? desensitized?) college classmate waved me over to come watch on her school-issued laptop during a break in business law 101 or something. It was a recording of a beheading of an American hostage, and his screams, the whole thing, was absolutely horrific. I wish I had turned away. I wish the school had filters to avoid that sort of thing in the first place.

What can your children see today on their school-issued devices and accounts, much less their personal devices and accounts? We'll get to that in the next chapter, as well as what you can do about it.

FOMO Is Real

Another thing that we've got to talk about regarding our kids, tech, and mental health is the concept of FOMO. If I had to pinpoint one feeling that social media platforms wanted us to feel based on what content they served to us, it would be FOMO.

Where everyone is (and you're not)
What everyone has (and you don't)
What everyone is doing (and you're missing)
What the ideal body looks like (and it's not yours)
What the ideal life looks like (yep, definitely not yours)
What the ideal job looks like (all gain, no pain)

This feeling has us all chasing the next best thing (and we aren't even sure what that is) instead of being content right where we are.

Let's look at some of the gamified features that push this FOMO narrative.

Within Snapchat there's something called Snap Maps that displays your child's live location with anybody that they're connected to, unless they're on ghost mode, and most kids don't stay on ghost mode.

(They'd be a lot happier and safer if they did, but they don't.)

Imagine you're in high school, and it's spring break, and you see that everybody is hanging out on the beautiful Gulf Coast of Florida (via Snap Maps) while you are chilling in your room on a staycation.

You then open Instagram and see your friends' stories documenting shenanigans that might "disappear" within 24 hours, but they are definitely seared into your memory, making you wish you could teleport there ASAP.

I get it. When Taylor Swift came to Atlanta, I didn't go. When I went online and saw everybody posting about going to her concert, dripping in friendship bracelets and glittery outfits, I felt FOMO. Now, I'm an adult, and I can deal with my adult choices of not spending a small fortune to go see someone perform. But with kids, it's a lot different.

When everybody is sharing their highlight reel and you're sitting at home watching it all unfold before your eyes, it does not feel good. At all.

The same idea of FOMO works as it relates to seeing what others are doing to themselves in terms of beauty or fashion. Children might see something and think "That looks a lot better than the real me."

But it's an illusion, right? If you're, let's say, an eighth-grade girl and you see a filter and think, oh my goodness, now I need plastic surgery, or now I need lip filler, or now I need to go to Sephora and get all this expensive makeup, or...fill in the blank. It's just not reality, it's draining their meager allowance/savings accounts, and it's hurting our children's self-esteem. Our children need confidence more than anything and, now more than ever, to sufficiently navigate this hyperconnected landscape.

On top of that, if all we are seeing is everybody's filtered, perfect lives, we're not seeing reality, so we then, understandably, feel bad about ourselves. Please be aware of what you're modeling to your children. If all you're posting about is *your* filtered life, you're not being honest with your followers or your friends, and your children will take note of your lack of authenticity. People rarely post if they are hurting, sad, or things aren't good. When you hop on this bandwagon, you're just contributing to that false narrative and not showing the full picture, and that's not a good model for your children. As I write this, I feel compelled to own up to the fact that I will often use the "Paris" filter on my Instagram Stories, a one-swipe "solution" to the wrinkles and acne scars that make me feel less beautiful. Even I am not immune and should maybe take my own advice.

One thing that's important and I like to emphasize to children who do have social media is that *happiness is an "unfollow" away*. I wish I could claim this gem as my own, but I need to attribute that insight to my dear friend and thought leader in this space, Tanner Clark of the *One Second of Strength* podcast.[6] Even as an adult in my forties, I have unfollowed some accounts that I just realized made me feel bad about myself. They weren't inherently negative, and some were overwhelmingly accomplished and positive in terms of their health, wellness, beauty, entrepreneurial, or design pursuits. But being constantly inundated with everyone's highs contributed to some of my very real lows. And so, unfollowing or hiding those accounts was the best course of action for my spirit.

Many of these influencers weren't doing anything wrong at all, but I would say certain fitness accounts and certain design accounts were just not great for my self-esteem. I would leave my feed feeling like, wow, I will never look like that or my house will never look like that. And so I decided to wish them all the best but unfollow them for my own sanity and mental health. And our children need to know that they can do the same and feel a lot better.

Choose Your Own (Healthier) Adventure

It helps to picture the use of technology either as an umbilical cord or as a viewing window. When we use technology consciously and proactively as a viewing window, we separate ourselves from the stimulation captured in that window. By observing through a viewing window, we can note that our own physical needs and wants are separate from what we see and make decisions based on that awareness while still using technology. We can operate playfully and thoughtfully.

When our connection to technology feels too much like an umbilical cord connection, we are likely to feel anxious or become disembodied—and shut down. We start to operate using the nervous system functioning that should be reserved for life-threatening situations.

Let's seriously contemplate helping our kids see tech as a tool to be utilized as a viewing window. Let's try to help our kids tune into their bodies and sense the power they have to control these viewing windows that exist at their fingertips. When they consider how they might best use technology to control stimulation at any given moment, they are less likely to become disembodied and more likely to function using their social engagement systems, which foster vitality without overwhelm.

Solutions Are Coming, But First

As we wrap this chapter, I want to remind you of the core ways that tech is impacting our children when it comes to their minds and spirits, both positively and negatively.

+ Enhanced creativity
+ Stronger connection to distant family/friends
– Decreased empathy (decreased face-to-face time has real implications on social awareness)
– Lower self-esteem
– Increased anxiety
– Decreased patience (due to tech's instant gratification)

– Reduced spiritual awareness (too much screen time can crowd out moments for mindfulness, reflection, or spiritual growth)

– Addiction risk

– Decreased resilience

~ Enhanced global awareness (this can be a + or –, depending on the content)

Now, without further ado, you will flip the page and get to Chapter 8, "Solutions: So What Do We Do?" It is time, and I'm so excited to be in this spot with you. Let's get to work.

Notes

1. Porges, S. and Buczynski, R. (n.d.). Polyvagal theory and trauma. *National Institute for the Clinical Application of Behavioral Medicine*. https://www.nicabm.com/topic/polyvagal-theory-explained/.

2. Porges, S. (n.d.). Polyvagal Theory. *National Institute for the Clinical Application of Behavioral Medicine*. https://www.nicabm.com/experts/stephen-porges/#:~:text=The%20theory%20centers%20around%20the, more%20sophisticated%20threat%2Dmitigation%20strategies.

3. McLeod, S. (2024). Erik Erikson's stages of psychosocial development. *Simply Psychology*. https://www.simplypsychology.org/erik-erikson.html.

4. MasterClass (2021). The Hays Code explained: history of Hollywood's Hays Code. *MasterClass*. https://www.masterclass.com/articles/hays-code-explained.

5. Gao, X., Pan, W., Chao, L. et al. (2017). Long-time exposure to violent video games does not show desensitization on empathy for pain: an fMRI study. *Frontiers in Psychology* 8. https://www.frontiersin.org/journals/psychology/articles/10.3389/fpsyg.2017.00650.

6. One Second of Strength podcast (n.d.). https://www.onesecondofstrength.com/podcast.

8 | Solutions: So What Do We Do?

I've been teasing this chapter for some time now, and I'm glad we are finally here. If you are anything like me, you want to solve problems ASAP instead of dwell on them. But sometimes having more context around the *why* before you jump into the *what* can be incredibly helpful to cast a full vision of the best solution. That is why this *entire book* led up to *this* chapter, instead of consisting solely of this chapter.

So what do we know?

- We know that things aren't great.
- We know that our children and young adults are struggling.
- We know that we all spend way too much time in front of screens.
- We know that parents, caregivers, teachers, administrators, and medical professionals are overwhelmed.
- We know that we've been manipulated, either inadvertently or deliberately and methodically, by big tech.
- We know that the current laws meant to protect consumers, and children, are decades out of date.
- We know that we can't keep going down this path.
- We know that we can't do it alone.

If we are going to change the trajectory of where we are, we need to start with candid conversations and an honest look at what we ourselves are modeling. What are we doing? How are we showing up for each other and our families?

The good news is there is hope in the tech tools out there, both free and paid, that can help you navigate parenting in a tech world. There is also hope in the multiple opportunities you have to communicate honestly and frequently with your children as they grow in this new era.

When I was growing up, I would say my mom and I had way more candid conversations about sex than I had with my dad. As you may have read in an earlier chapter—or you may have skipped that part to get to this chapter—I grew up in a divorced household, with lovely parents, and I'm friends with them still to this day, and they're friends with each other.

But I think the only thing my dad ever said to me about sex was "You're not dating until you're 30." That wasn't very helpful. So we shouldn't necessarily take notes from our parents about how often or how detailed we get about what our children are encountering online. Our parents might not have been the best models because they didn't have to parent in the same kind of world as we do. We've got to be talking with our kids openly, honestly, candidly, and more frequently than probably either we or our kids would like to, and we need to have those discussions earlier than we might think is necessary because they have more access to unmoderated information than we ever did.

Even if your children don't have any Internet access whatsoever, do they go to a public or private school? Do they ride a school bus? Do they hang out with other kids who have access or have older siblings? It's not a matter of if, but when, they're going to be exposed to mature themes, not just sexual themes, but just mature themes in general, whether it's what's happening in the news today or violence or just about anything else in the adult world. And **you** need to be their source of wisdom and truth and their safe space. Not TikTok.

And if they know that they can come to you and you'll remain calm, that goes a long way toward keeping them safe. It's also so important to get *your* head out of the sand. Please don't think "not my kid" or "my kid would never"; good kids make bad choices. They're children—the frontal lobes of their brains are not fully formed until they're in their early twenties. They're not physiologically capable of fully mature, rational thought or action, and that's why they need their parents' guidance, and that's why we need to be there for them and give them some grace, especially because we've handed them supercomputers way before they're fully ready to manage that responsibility.

This chapter of the book is meant to be the guidebook I wish I had when my son was born. This is where you'll find my recommendations and suggestions. This is where you get to take a hard look in the mirror and decide how your children will be protected in this information age.

So what do we do?

Start by Surfacing It

Talk to Other Parents

Do you have a neighborhood group, a local Wait Until 8th chapter,[1] a book club, or parent–teacher organization/association (PTO/PTA)? Collective action begins with small, empowered, passionate groups. Never underestimate the power of parents motivated to protect their children. Ever.

Talk to Your Child's Pediatrician

Some of the most powerful insights I've gained into how this new tech landscape is affecting children is by talking to those healthcare heroes who are on the front lines. To hear firsthand how the rate of children coming to emergency rooms who have either successfully or unsuccessfully attempted to die by suicide has significantly increased over the past decade—from the doctors tasked with saving their lives—will break your heart. One pediatrician told me at a recent school tech night that 30% of her day is now spend evaluating and diagnosing mental health related issues versus in the past where a typical office visit was spent examining a peculiar rash or diagnosing a rough sounding cough.

Talk to Your Child's Teachers and School Administrators

If your child's school provides (or even mandates) school-issued tech, they have a duty to make sure that tech is safe for your children to use on campus. What does that mean? It means children should be able to safely search, play educational interactive games, and learn without encountering problematic content (like pornography) and dangerous people (like predators).

If they require your children to take that tech home for homework, research, or collaboration purposes, they are responsible for making sure the tech can be safer at home as well or unlocked enough so that you can add your own parental controls to it. Any other arrangement is unacceptable.

Talk to Their Coaches, Youth Leaders, and Instructors

Please do not feel that you have to cave to unrealistic or unhealthy expectations from other influential adults in your child's life, *especially* if they want your children to join a social media platform for communication purposes before they are 13 years old.

Talk to Your Local Legislators

Call them. Write letters. Visit their offices. Attend hearings. We have to advocate for safer laws to help protect our most vulnerable as the current ones aren't cutting it.

Join My Facebook Group

You can talk to more than half a million other parents and caregivers across the globe who are experiencing this dynamic right alongside you by joining the "Parenting in a Tech World" group on Facebook.

Then Own It

You are not an ostrich, so get your head out of the sand. So many of us, myself included, think we will just know when our child is struggling. We think our child would never do x, y, or z, but as I've said multiple times (it bears repeating) *good kids make bad choices.* We all did as children and adolescents. Ironically, as I'm writing this chapter I have church streaming on YouTube in the background, and one of my favorite pastors (Joel Thomas of North Point Community Church) just said, "You owe it to yourself to be honest with yourself." Nailed it.

30,000-Foot View

So now let's zoom out. We've been in the weeds, and now it's time to get an aerial view of the situation. Outside of the relational aspects both internally (at home) and externally (at school, on the go, with friends), it's time to look at the multiple access points.

Boots on the Ground

As you're going through this process, if you have older children and you are working to dial some of the access back, it's going to be a bit painful. That doesn't mean it's not worth doing. In these instances, feel free to be vulnerable with your children. Explain that you made some mistakes as their parent, one of which was allowing too much too soon, and you need to do what's in their best interest. Tell them directly: "I want the best for you." Then invite them to join you on this journey by asking "Will you trust me and navigate this with me?" Much like the first step of any major journey can feel painful and overwhelming, it really does take putting one "boot" in front of the other and soon, you will have made *so* much progress!

Conversations

Nothing can replace open and honest conversations with your children—much earlier than you might think, more frequently than you might think, and much younger than you might think you need to have certain conversations about heavy, important topics.

What to Talk About (and When and How)

What: FOMO—fear of missing out, discussed more in depth in the previous chapter.

When: Any time *you* feel it, before you let your child access social media to prep them for what's to come, and then every few weeks or so once they have access.

How: Share a story with them that you recall from your younger days of feeling left out, and ask them if they have ever felt that way or if they have ever hesitated about sharing something online because they didn't want others to feel left out.

What: Filtered life versus real life—talk openly with them about how *you* feel after consuming content online, and point out the inconsistencies with curated lives versus the real story.

When: Any time you encounter it and your children are around and you want to have a thoughtful discussion.

How: Point out the nuances of what you share online and if you ever hold anything back or filter or hide anything. For example, "I'm about to post this picture of our holiday decorations to Instagram, but what

I'm not showing is the laundry pile on the sofa. Isn't it interesting how we don't see the full picture of people's lives online?"

What: "Happiness is an unfollow away" (shout out to @realtannerclark for that phrase)—discuss the power of algorithms and how we must proactively curate our digital experiences (as they are most certainly curated for us).

When: Any time you encounter feeling not so great after spending time online, and your children are around, and you want to have a thoughtful discussion.

How: As you are scrolling through your feed, if you see something that doesn't sit well with you, show your child how you block/unfollow/report certain accounts and content so that the algorithms learn what to *not* show you.

What: Sexting—as there are legal consequences for the possession and distribution of child sexual abuse material (CSAM).

When: Whenever your children are old enough to operate a device that can take a picture or video of themselves or another minor.

How: Please start early and let young children know that while it's fun to take pictures, we never take (or send) pictures or videos of our body parts that live under our bathing suits. Never, ever, ever.

What: Slang—both words and emoji.

When: Whenever your children are old enough to read, write, and communicate digitally.

How: Much like children learn that words have multiple meanings—like the bark on a tree or the bark of a dog—help them understand that their words hold a great deal of power. Words can bring us closer together and words can tear us apart. Be sure to review Chapter 11 to get a comprehensive lowdown on the latest slang.

What: Passwords—to everything!

When: As soon as your children are old enough to understand what a password is and memorize a sequence of numbers or letters.

How: My favorite analogy to use when this conversation comes up is as follows: a responsible parent wouldn't give someone under the age of 18 their very own apartment and only one key to that apartment. The same thing applies to their tech.

What: Screen time—and all that entails such as consumption, creation, competition, curation, connection, quality over quantity.

When: As soon as your child can ask for it.

How: In addition to demonstrating a healthy relationship with screens, and we will talk about modeling in just a moment, it helps when children are going to have more access to screens frequently to sit down together and review a tech contract together. There is a free, customizable one provided in Chapter 12, "Resources."

Speaking of **what, when,** and **how,** if you are struggling with discussing *any* of these issues with your child, please do not hesitate to reach out to a licensed healthcare professional like your child's pediatrician or a licensed marriage and family therapist (LMFT) or their school counselor to give you guidance. Every child and every situation are different.

Modeling

It is imperative that we model appropriate tech behavior for our children. If they see how we balance the demands (of work and social lives) and desires (to passively scroll, to play video games) that impact us via technology, they can learn how to thrive in a hyperconnected world with fewer lectures.

Additionally, at some point your child is going to encounter problematic content or people online. It's not a matter of *if* but when. So, when that happens, please freak out quietly, give yourself some grace, take a deep breath, and make sure they know that you are a safe place.

Note: This does not mean you must condone certain unhealthy behaviors or that there are not consequences for their actions. What it *does* mean is that you are there to support your child and help them navigate this rocky landscape of growing up online. You aren't meant to remove every jagged boulder from their path, but you are there to guide, love, and protect.

Babies in the first few days, weeks, and months of their development thrive in environments that prioritize skin-to-skin contact and quality face time so they can pick up on expressions.

With the advent of smartphones, parents started spending less of these critical moments bonding with their children and instead, capturing these moments digitally and then getting distracted by notifications, emails, texts, and social media.

We have more pictures of children now in their first month of being alive on this planet than we used to have of one human for their entire life. The amount of media—photos and videos—we are capturing is mind-blowing. The average human has far too many photos and videos on their camera roll. We need to spend more time living in the moment instead of trying to capture and document each moment.

When our children are young and see us scrolling instead of connecting with other humans in real life, it leaves a lasting impression.

Ask yourself what you're really doing on your phone.

Once all those work emails are checked and attended to, and urgent/important texts from family or close friends addressed, what else is a priority?

We all know that social media remains pretty high up on the list despite not being that important, along with games, select video content, and music.

I highly encourage all of us to take a look at our screen time usage reports where we can see what percentage of time we spend in each app. Pretty eye-opening. That's time we will never get back with our kids. Sorry/not sorry that I went there.

A lot of us feel like we can't even breathe or function without our smartphones. It's like another limb. And so what does that convey to our children? Can we leave the home without our smartphone or our smart watch? Can we have dinner with each other without constantly looking at our phone?

Try to put it on silent, turn it over, or turn off notifications. If our children come into our room at night and we have our significant other with us, are we both just scrolling on our phones while the TV is also on, or are we talking with each other and laughing and loving and hugging? You know what I mean? There's just so much that our children pick up from just watching how we interact with our tech before they even get their own tech.

And that's critical.

Timing

What is the right age to give my child a smartphone? And should I go with a smart watch first? What about a tablet? What about social media? These are such a nuanced questions—the right time for access and in what capacity—that I decided to address it in-depth in Chapter 10, "Q (and More Importantly, A)." It's the most frequently asked question I've received over the course of my career. What I will say here is that "delay is the way" (full credit to Chris McKenna of Protect Young Eyes for that profound statement). I have never met a parent who regretted delaying access, and I have met so many parents who live with regrets to this very day because of too much access too soon, myself included. Please know that your children will pull on your heartstrings knowing your desire for them to not be left out. But there are some things that you want them to be left out of. Like bullying. And toxic rabbit holes.

Tools

See also Chapter 12, "Resources," but essentially, you need to protect their hearts, their minds, their bodies, your relationship with them, the Internet that comes into your home, and the devices they access. Where to start?

Let's start with your home and let's think in terms of layers.

Layer 1: Network

How Does the Internet Get into Your Home?   Once you identify who your Internet service provider (ISP) is, it's time to see what parental controls (time limits and content filters) they offer. A quick Google search plus the name of your ISP should render that information for you, as well as a call to their customer service hotline. Don't be shy! They should be well-versed on how to ensure a safer experience for your family. In fact, we as a society should demand that the Internet they bring into our homes is inherently safe unless we work to unlock access to more mature themes—not vice versa.

Additionally, a safer router (like the Gryphon) or a device that connects to your existing router (like the Bark Home) can help make this experience much easier for you to manage, given that these companies are focused on family safety first. The Bark Home is a small device that plugs into your home's Wi-Fi router, and it works by allowing or not allowing content at different times.

The Bark Home's Internet parental controls work by allowing you to block websites and apps and set screen time schedules on your child's home devices—things like TVs, tablets, gaming consoles, and computers. It works on phones—iOS and Android—too. With the Bark Home, you can also help protect your family from potentially inappropriate content like pornography, gaming sites, and excessive violence. You can set up schedules where your kid can only access the Internet on these devices at certain times, like after dinner or only on weekends. It's up to you.

Network-level Internet parental controls can give you peace of mind that your child is not getting into anything they shouldn't, which is the perfect way to help keep them safe online and in real life.

Layer 2: Device

What Devices Within Your Home (Mobile and Connected) Can Access the Internet? If your ISP cannot connect to a piece of tech, perhaps because it's using LTE (wireless data) and not Wi-Fi, that's when you will need to rely on app-based parental controls (like the Bark App in addition to built-in device-level controls like Google FamilyLink or Apple's screen time—more details on these in the following sections) as an additional layer.

Tip: Don't forget about smart televisions, gaming consoles, and that tech drawer with old smartphones, tablets, or laptops that have not yet been recycled or donated.

Content Monitoring with Bark   The Bark App, launched in 2015, uses advanced machine learning and statistical analysis techniques to recognize potential problems. Simple keyword searches are not enough to detect the majority of issues, which is why Bark's parental control app uses contextual analysis and natural language processing to determine when something serious might be happening.

For example, Bark knows the difference between a kid saying "This homework makes me wanna kill myself," versus "Nobody cares about me!! I wanna kill myself." Bark's algorithm also keeps up with the latest in teen slang.

Screen Time Management and Website Blocking with Bark   Families can manage not only when their kids can access the Internet on their devices but also which sites and apps they can visit.

You can create custom profiles for each child in your house, create screen time schedules, and manage access to a wide variety of websites including video streaming, gaming, adult content, and more.

With Bark, you can manage your children's screen time from your own phone via the Bark app or website, regardless of whether you have an iPhone and your kids have an Android (or vice versa).

In terms of web filtering, Apple's Screen Time and Google Family Link web filters only block general content. Bark, on the other hand, breaks down a wide range of categories and exceptions to enable a more customized and refined level of protection.

Now Let's Look Even Closer at Mobile Devices   What devices don't need Internet to connect to the entire world? Smartphones, smart watches, and tablets like the iPad that can connect to a cellular network are all able to access the outside world without a Wi-Fi network or password.

This is where device-level protections come in as an additional layer on top of the network level protections:

Google FamilyLink: If your child has Android devices, this is the "family parental controls service by Google that allows parents to adjust parameters for their children's devices. The application allows parents to restrict content, approve or disapprove apps, set screen times, and more" (https://en.wikipedia.org/wiki/Google_Family_Link). It's free, decent, and while there is some friction around Google deciding that a child is basically capable of adult choices at age 13, it does a good job of working in the way you intend.

Apple Families: If you visit apple.com/families, you will see a great deal of fluff when it comes to their purported parental controls. Don't fall for the hype. Of all the parental control offerings, I would say that Apple's are the most widely adopted yet most frustrating. I'll get to that in just a moment. The only good thing I can say about Apple's parental controls is that they are free, if and when they work.

Bark: I've outlined many advantages of using both the Bark Home and Bark App, but I will add one more thing here: advanced content monitoring (ACM). This is important, and no other company does it like Bark. ACM is the reason Bark is able to send timely alerts to parents and caregivers about the dangers living deep in a child's digital signal. ACM is the reason Bark has been able to save children's lives. ACM is the reason I decided to work at Bark and not another tech company. It's a truly unique capability that uses a proprietary data set that gets smarter every day. Bark is the most comprehensive one-stop shop when it comes to holistic parental controls, from location tracking to website blocking and everything in between.

A Note About Apple   Ask any Internet safety expert who understands the issues facing children today, and 90% of them will tell you that Apple products are not the best products for children.

Note: I say that writing to you from a MacBook Air wearing an Apple Watch and having an iPhone right by my side distracting me every five minutes or so. But I am an adult. Apple prioritizes privacy, *not* child safety, which is great for adults and not great for children who need guidance.

Not only that, but Apple's screen time features have bugs in them.

The *Wall Street Journal*, TechCrunch, and Mashable have all covered the ongoing issues with Apple's parental controls. Essentially, even if you set time limits for children on Apple devices, children can circumvent them because of the software bugs and not because you did anything wrong.

Thousands of parents have lamented that they will set filters to try to prevent their children from encountering explicit or certain types of content but because of Apple's bugs, the children can still access that content. Again, this is not because the parent messed up somehow but because Apple hasn't prioritized fixing the bugs or known workarounds for their most vulnerable users.

Additionally, there are concerns with the safety and ethics surrounding Apple's iCloud. Meant to back up pictures and photos, the platform has been hacked, and that's not even my biggest gripe. What most consumers don't know is that Apple made plans to detect and remove any CSAM, but ultimately decided to not proceed with those plans. And I just can't think of any reason why it would be okay to keep that sort of content on iCloud when you can remove it. Pedophiles do not deserve privacy, and children deserve justice. But here we are.

Don't take my word for it—just look at the work of Heat Initiative. Through their site protectchildrennotabuse.org, they are calling on all of us to demand that Apple[2]:

> *Let kids report abuse*
> *Create easily accessible reporting in iMessage for kids and parents to report inappropriate images and harmful situations.*
> *Require safer apps*
> *Ensure that only age-appropriate, safe apps are made available to and advertised to children.*

Stop the spread of child sexual abuse

Stop the storage and spread of known child sexual abuse images and videos in iCloud.

These are not unrealistic, hard-to-implement demands. Certainly not for one of the largest, most profitable global companies.

I know a lot of kids want Apple—it's sleek. They have great branding and features and billion-dollar marketing budgets, but a lot of kids also want a Ferrari. That doesn't mean you get them one for their first car.

Please consider any other option besides Apple products for a child's first device.

(And yes, that includes the Apple Watch and iPad.)

Androids are much safer for children.

The Bark Phone (an Android device) is the best, safest smartphone choice for a child.

The Bark Watch is the best, safest smart watch for a child.

And if you don't want to go with the Bark Phone or Watch, that's totally fine.

There are many fine options out there!

Gabb, Troomi, Gizmo, the Light Phone, flip phones—they are all better than Apple. I would pick literally any other smartphone for a child before going with an iPhone. Just say no to Apple devices for kids until Apple cleans up its act.

Layer 3: In-App and In-Game Parental Controls This chapter is already so long, and rightfully so given what needs to take place to keep your children safer online and healthier in real life. But, for the sake of space and sanity, I'm *not* going to go over every parental control setting for every single app your child might want to use or game they like to play. What I will do is let you know that there are options, and before you let your child use any app or play any game, *please* Google what they want to access plus "parental controls" and then implement them. I beg of you.

Another important step here is to make sure your child can't just download any app or game without your permission. *Ask to buy* is a beautiful concept and a critical safety layer.

Once children have already downloaded an app, at least on Apple devices, even if you make them delete it from a device, they can redownload it without asking for your permission again. I was going to add this to the Apple rant section, but it deserved to be here instead.

Finally, in Chapter 12, "Resources," I will give you so many links and options for how to set these up in more detail.

Layer 4: Location   Location is everything and not just in real estate. If I could give one powerful, free, and easy tip to all parents and caregivers, it would be to not allow connected tech in bedrooms, bathrooms, or behind closed doors.

Period.

End of story.

Be Curious

Caroline Gebhardt (the family and child mental health counselor mentioned several times in this book) suggests looking beyond the surface and more into what's truly driving a child's desire to play an online game or escaping to a video or movie.

"As a mom of three boys ranging in age from young teen to preschooler, their desire for screens is strong, and we all feel the peer pressure of '*but he gets to play that such-and-such online game!*' but I measure the allotment with mindfulness," she said.

First, become curious about the technology: Ask yourself, "Are my kids searching for something for knowledge about a subject? Or are they traveling down rabbit holes of potential dangers?"

Then, get into the details: "What kind of games are they playing, and are those games a swap for something they could embody in real life? Or is the fantasy of gaming a way to explore a mythic voyage, and yet at what point does that create more dissociation or disembodiment?"

Whether it's an Internet search or a gaming device, she suggests paying attention to their desire and their reach and then remembering to recognize her place as her children's holding environment to provide the limits she sets around screen use.

Gebhardt mentioned how this situation will quickly make you neither the most loved parent in the house for a few minutes nor the most popular parent in the neighborhood, but don't let what the kids think of you get to you. You are their parent, not their friend.

She continued, "I know kids need limits. Kids push into their parents to find themselves. Boundaries keep us safe. Knowing it takes at least the first three decades of life for full brain development, I consider it a practice to stay the steady, predictable limit setter who can help my children ride through all their feelings whether they love me in the moment or not."

Make a Tech Contract

As you're trying to figure out how to navigate parenting in a tech world, it's really helpful to have a tech contract. If you have older children, I get it: if you try to print out a tech contract and put it on a fridge, they might roll their eyes. But for younger children, when they still listen to you and care about what you have to say, a tech contract can be really helpful to outline the major responsibility that comes with access to this type of tool.

And it can help set boundaries and set guidelines for what we will do and what we won't do with technology and what the ramifications are if we don't follow these rules. It's a lot easier to point to a physical piece of paper hanging on our refrigerator and say, "Hey, we did not follow this, and here's the consequence."

Good news—I have a free one you can customize in Chapter 12.

Support Legislation

It's important to support legislation that holds big tech companies accountable, as current laws are sorely outdated.

One such piece of legislation that we should all be paying attention to is Sammy's Law (named after Sammy, who will forever be 16).

Sammy was able to purchase what he thought was a benign pill via Snapchat, but it had fentanyl in it. It was delivered to his home as quickly and easily as a pizza, and he died.

If Sammy's Law would have existed, his family could have had a monitoring solution (like Bark) connected to their son's Snapchat account that would've alerted them to this drug solicitation and delivery.

And he would still be here.

And so would so many other children that have died as a result of social media harms.

Please keep an eye out for effective legislation bubbling up at both the state and federal levels. In addition to the proposed changes to Kids Online Safety Act (KOSA) that may or may not pass by the time you read this book, we've got to continue to hold tech CEOs accountable—not just Mark Zuckerberg, but everyone.

The most helpful legislation would give parents the ability to opt in to protect their kids. Whether it's through your Internet service provider, your cellular service provider, whatever device your child has access to, or whatever social media platforms your child visits, safety solutions exist right now that can help protect your child from most of the bad while letting in the good.

But unfortunately, platforms, gaming consoles, apps, and other devices aren't required to offer adequate safety solutions nor are they legally held accountable for the harms that children encounter while using these products.

We have the power to remove that blocker.

If parents want to opt in, let parents use these safety solutions. Much like we have with video doorbells and carbon monoxide detectors: we can opt in for those safety solutions. We can opt for safer car seats right now. But parents are currently very limited in what they can opt for when it comes to universal parental controls. The majority of parents are stuck with what the platform or the device gives them. And what we know, based on data, is that's not enough.

We need to let parents protect and give parents the ability to opt in to make their children safer and ultimately, save their children's lives.

For-profit companies have got to do more to keep the most vulnerable users safe on their platforms. There's plenty of time for these children to use those platforms when they're older without jeopardizing the one precious childhood they have.

Be Aware of App Features

Here's the deal—there are "riskier" apps out there than this book has pages to cover. That said, there are some common features that make apps and games inherently risky—despite what brand they live under or what app rating they might have.

Here is a comprehensive list of features that live within a growing list of apps and games that can pose risks to kids while being generally safe for adults:

- Messaging capabilities
- Gif/emoji communication
- Live video chat (1:1)
- Live video chat (group)
- Disappearing text
- Disappearing photos
- Disappearing videos
- Location sharing
- Location tracking
- Ability to send payments
- In-app purchases
- Ability to send gifts
- Browsers
- Hashtags (or searchable content)
- Push notifications
- Anonymous features
- Algorithms
- Third-party integrations
- Suggested friends to connect with or popular accounts to follow
- User-generated content
- AI (artificially intelligent) chatbots

That is an exhaustive list! As you read through it, did an app come to mind that you hadn't previously considered? Did you hesitate to understand why any of these features made it to the list? I bet if you asked your children about the apps and games they love, you might be surprised to realize that some of these features exist within those platforms. Remember, though—don't freak out. File that information away, and have those important conversations.

Unsolicited Nudes Sent. Now What?

Here's what happens if you ever find unsolicited pictures on your child's phone. First, when addressing this, you remain calm. If they proactively bring this to your attention, you say, "Thank you so much, thank you for telling me. That's a really mature decision. Let's figure out how to navigate this together. You're not in trouble. You did not do anything wrong. Even if you enjoyed talking with them, even if you sent them photos back, you're still a child, and it's not your fault."

Additionally, you might need to say, depending on their age and stage, "Let's get you the help that you need in terms of talking to a professional who has helped other children navigate this issue. We might also need to preserve this evidence, but first, let's reach out to law enforcement to let them know what's happening."

Next, what you need to do is preserve the evidence but under the direction of skilled law enforcement professionals so that you aren't further capturing or spreading CSAM. So before blocking the sender, which you should later do, take screenshots of things like their account and profile information and direct messages to provide to law enforcement. Ideally, you can arm law enforcement with enough information so that the predator or offender stops contacting you and stops contacting the hundreds of other children they're contacting as well.

I say to contact local law enforcement first because often, if you were to reach out to a platform first, they might inevitably tip off the predator causing them to go dark or create a new account and keep offending. Again, always let law enforcement know first, follow their instructions, and then block.

Moving forward, make sure that your child has the appropriate therapy that they need. Don't hesitate to reach out to your child's pediatrician or school counselor to assess what level of care they might need. There's also the National Center for Missing and Exploited Children (NCMEC).

The NCMEC has a website called Take It Down. If your child unfortunately has nude photos or videos online, NCMEC can help them get it taken down. Unfortunately, social media platforms don't always respond quickly to those requests, which is why we need the Take It Down site in the first place.

What else do you need to do? Make sure you don't have any personally identifiable information (PII) about you on your public profiles. What you as an adult put out into the world can absolutely come back to harm your children. Less PII is more.

Pictures can give you more information than you realize. Think about a picture in your bio where someone is wearing a school uniform with a school logo on it or an image of a family holiday photo in front of your house. Maybe there's an address number visible on the house?

AI also complicates things. Today, you can upload a photo and use an algorithm to tell you with precision where that photo was taken. The moral of the story is the less you put online about yourself, the smaller the digital footprint that you curate.

That's why I suggest always using a discerning eye when you upload anything so as not to provide any help to any possible bad actors.

Know Your Ratings

Pay attention to the ratings on the video games you buy or apps you allow your children to download. Just like movies, the gaming industry in particular has tried to help parents make better decisions for their children, so they know a little about the content inside those games. The Entertainment Software Rating Board (ESRB) describes itself as the "nonprofit, self-regulatory body for the video game industry." ESRB tries to help parents make informed choices about what games they should allow their children to play based on their respective family values. App ratings are a bit more ambiguous. There is no independent regulatory body that is held accountable for what an app is rated versus what an app actually exposes you to, but that will ideally change with updated legislation.

Vet Sources

Teach your children about misinformation and vetting sources. As someone who was responsible for writing the news that was broadcast every week for a portion of time on my local NBC affiliate, I realize just how fragile the media ecosystem is. I have biases, I don't know everything, and I'm culling my information from sources that may or may not have biases. Unless your source of truth is the single source of truth, know that there is always room for interpretation. Teach your kids that.

Long-Form Video Content

If you're going to allow kids to watch things, it should be long-form educational, professionally produced content with a clear purpose. Now let's break that down. Long form means it's a half-hour or more, not 30 seconds or three minutes. The content should be thoughtfully produced by professionals dedicated to creating content with an educational goal, and not user-generated low-quality content. Ideally, when children consume this content, it's via a large, nonmobile screen so that, as a parent, you can see what they're actually doing and watching.

Be a CAN-Doer

As a parent, it's easy to beat yourself up over what you can't do. But I'd suggest working on all the things you CAN do.

When the *Today* Show calls and needs me to go talk about keeping children safer online? I can do it. Not because of me. I'm a human. I make mistakes. I'm imperfect.

But I believe in a higher power that keeps me going every day. It's why I have eternal, infinite hope that anything can happen. And I wake up every day with that hope, knowing that, if there are problems to solve, why not me? Why not now?

Because I can.

I can do all things through Christ who strengthens me.

I can deal with my parents' divorce.

I can overcome childhood sexual abuse.

I can defeat crippling anxiety and depression.

I can endure mean kids.

I can get into a private, prestigious Catholic high school despite not being a legacy or Catholic.

I can survive a great deal of bad college decisions all by the grace of God because he has a plan for me to be on this planet beyond 2001.

I can quit all the bad things.

I can make very tough but healthy decisions to leave (what I thought was) my whole world at the time in order to gain a better perspective on what's really important in this world.

I can take time off from college and nanny twin six-month-old babies.

I can go back to school and get my BBA in marketing.

I can rise quickly from an intern at the top radio station in Atlanta to the youngest account executive in just two years.

I can survive a terrifying relapse and quit all the bad things again.

I can survive childbirth and postpartum depression and anxiety.

I can have the courage to not return to my promising career.

I can start a new one.

I can write the difficult story.

I can fly solo across the country to tell that story to a room of 400 people.

I can go back to work full-time in tech despite not having a technical degree.

I can ask for what I'm worth.

I can be a C-level executive.

I can fly across the country again to appear on *The Doctors*.

I can host a television show on my local NBC affiliate station.

I can leave a toxic work environment despite not knowing what's next.

I can write this book.

I can begin again.

And again.

And again.

Until he calls me home.

And *you* can be an educated, empowered, effective parent in a tech world! You don't have to do it alone.

If you are overwhelmed by what you just read in this lengthy chapter, that's completely normal and understandable. It's a lot. It's frankly a full-time job just to keep a child safer online these days. Chapter 12 provides next steps and a wealth of information (and people who will hold your hand every step of the way).

But please, raise your hand so we can see you and **help you**.

Notes

1. Wait Until 8th home page. https://www.waituntil8th.org/.
2. Protect Children Not Abuse home page. https://protectchildrenno tabuse.org/.

9 | Final Thoughts

When I was in fifth grade, around 1990, recycling education was a *big* thing. Almost everyone was on board, and I remember the promise and hope everyone had to help avoid global warming. Basically, the collective thought was that "If you do these things, recycle, turn off lights, bike versus drive, etc. we can save the planet." That meant clean air and water (a fundamental right if you ask me) in the future, a time that seemed so far away, where we'd all be flying solar-powered cars and talking on video phones.

Well, we've gotten the video phone aspect right.

As we arrive at the end of this book, I'm filled with (cautiously optimistic) hope. This is my "If we all recycle, we can save the planet" moment. And I do believe, in short, if we can just take some of the actions outlined here, the kids will be alright. Because, like I said earlier, no parent in the history of parenting on this planet has ever had to deal with what we're dealing with. But we're getting by. We're making progress. We're getting better at all of this. We are learning the truth and advocating for what's best for our children.

Regardless of your approach to how you want to lead your child into and through the tech world, you'll want to find a personal philosophy that works for you and your family and **hold firm** to it.

I can't stress that enough—the hold firm part.

You know what's best for your child, despite what outside influences suggest. Those outside influences will only get louder as they get older, and you may grow weary of having the same old screen time and social media back and forth, but please: *hold firm*.

As I reflect on my own experiences, there are certainly things that I wish I had done better. But I cannot go back in time. My son is now in his teens, so I do have a few more years before he's out of the house, but in many aspects that ship has sailed.

At times, I wish I could go back to when he was a baby or a toddler or early elementary or later elementary or middle school (during a pandemic, what a gut punch)—I'd take a redo on any of those precious fleeting years before high school.

Speaking of surviving an unprecedented global pandemic as two working parents with an only child, although nobody could have planned for that situation, there are many things we could have done better.

Hindsight is 20/20 and sometimes surreal.

I'm not the only parent struggling with this, and studies reflect what we still grapple with. One such study post-pandemic found that even when public health precautions were lifted, screen time did not decrease back to prepandemic levels.[1]

As I look back at the choices I made (or didn't make), I am struck by a lack of clarity on why I wasn't stronger. Why didn't I say no? Why didn't I delay social media or gaming or screen use overall? I wish future Titania could have shaken then Titania with the knowledge she (I) has now.

I'm convinced now that I was too worried about my son liking me and focused on his immediate "happiness" versus what sustainable, healthy satisfaction looks like. I was also tired and overwhelmed. I needed a break, and screens were a quick fix that kept him in one place, mostly quiet (unless he was gaming with others), and under the "safety" of our roof. In a way, I was being his friend instead of his parent. I was also appealing to both his and my desire to be accepted, and not left out. In hindsight, I needed to *ensure he was left out* (of the bad things like toxic group text threads, harmful TikTok algorithms, and YouTube influencers spreading misinformation) while making sure he was included in actual, uplifting interpersonal experiences. (For more information about the harm TikTok can cause, see "Attorney General Schwalb Sues TikTok for Preying on District Children, Operating an Illegal Virtual Economy" on the website for the Office of the Attorney General for the District of Columbia.[2])

For crying out loud, I'm a professional who works in this space. I'm supposed to be an expert, an authority. I didn't think some of these things would happen to him without me having a solid heads up.

But they did. And that's something that I'll leave for him to share if and when he chooses to.

Suffice to say, many of the issues that my very own company works to alert parents to are things that my son and his peer group encountered that I didn't know were happening until Bark brought them to my attention.

I really thought he would come and talk to me. I'm an open mom. I'm a cool mom. (So is every mom ever, right?) But I really am. I understand this landscape. I'm calm.

And I know when my child should or shouldn't be exposed to certain things. I know it happens all too frequently and know my first reaction shouldn't be to yell, freak out, or judge. My role as a mother, as a caregiver, is to guide him and help him figure out what to do next.

But even then, being fully "in the know," I was completely blindsided and left in the dark for much longer than I should have been. It hurts. It's shocking. It's overwhelming at times. But now that I'm on the other side of it—I have so much more clarity. And with this experience, at least I can help you avoid being in that same exact position.

I didn't have a book like this to read when my son was younger. I made all the mistakes when it came to raising him in a tech world. I let him play on an iPad with no parental controls. I let him watch too much YouTube and television when I should have been pushing him to play outside, read, draw, or just be bored. I pacified him at restaurants and doctor's appointments and during conference calls with the easiest and most addictive tool I had in my parenting toolbox: a screen. I said yes to certain games and apps before I was ready because "all of his friends" had access.

I told you many of my personal stories. I told you about my monster. We also know that other monsters are out there. And we know now how monsters can take so many different forms, from the online predator to the bully to the former friend to the new lover to the social media company to the big tech manufacturer to the addictive algorithm to the lack of sleep to the lobbyist working to prevent meaningful legislation from moving forward.

Regardless of the monsters I've listed here, we can choose to always be there for our children.

When they are babies, you will both love that special time, so put down that phone when they are awake. I know this sounds drastic. But they know. They know when they're looking at you and you're not looking at them.

There's actually a term for it: *phubbing*. When someone is on a screen in your presence instead of being present with you—that's phubbing. Don't phub your babies.

When they are toddlers, grab that phone and capture a few things, but again, put the phone away, live their life *with* them—you do not need to document it all behind a lens.

When they are in grade school, keep living in the real world. Introduce them to as many experiences as you can. Have tech-free playdates. Model work–life balance. They have the rest of their lives to get immersed in the grind of being tethered to email and work and research and spreadsheets. Don't let their memory of you be 90% that.

Show them all that life has to offer while you're leaning in to what's best for their physical and mental health. Introduce them to things that stimulate all their senses and both the right and left hemispheres of their brain, including movement. Shy away from things that lead to addiction, whether it's sugar or screens. The mantra of moderation and "less is more" applies here. Be there to catch their annoyance and anger and admiration and frustration. Really, really be there. They will not like some of you rules, and that's okay.

When your kids are old enough to have sleepovers, and I realize they are a fun aspect childhood, please default to making sure your house is the sleepover house so you can remain in more control. I can't tell you how many horror stories I've heard that involve children and sleepovers. They are rarely a great idea. Consider having a rule for devices entering your home if kids come over: they put them in a basket, and they don't go behind closed doors. Children should be focused on enjoying childhood, not the world through a filter or algorithm.

Make sure all your Wi-Fi networks (if you have more than one in your home) have passwords that only you know. Refrain from giving your child the password to the Wi-Fi network. You are the gatekeeper. You must be in charge of the monitoring and filtering. That is critical. Kids can't access the Internet when they can't get on the Internet (unless they have a device with cellular network connectivity, and that's when you need additional screen time controls and/or rules around location of those devices).

Parenting mistakes impact 100% of parents but nevertheless can cause such shame. I have so many regrets, and I can't go back in time for a do-over.

I hope that, after reading this, you will not have to live with the same regrets I do.

I want to tell my 8-year-old self to speak up and stop him from hurting anyone else.

I want to tell my 17-year-old self to take computer programming more seriously. It could be quite lucrative *cough*Facebook*cough*.

I want to shake my 19-year-old self straight and impress on my cloudy brain that just because everyone else is doing it doesn't mean it's a good choice. And go to class for Pete's sake. And go back to church while you're at it. And call your mother back; she's paying for your cell phone, you jerk.

I want to tell my 21-year-old self that you will still be paying that student loan off when you are 31. And go to law school. Or Parsons School of Design. Or Savannah College of Art and Design.

I want to tell my 24-year-old self that one more time actually can hurt. A lot. With forever repercussions.

I want to tell my 32-year-old self that my son needs me as his parent first and his friend later.

But I can't.

When my son is older, and in his youthful prime, will he hear my pleading to be all and do all that he can with his God-given talents and gifts? Or will he just think I'm a nag?

God, I pray for the former.

I am so thankful to have made it through multiple rocky periods and am now using every single second to grow, learn, love, connect, help, and flourish.

Yesterday is history, tomorrow is a mystery, and today is a gift; that's why they call it the present.

—*Eleanor Roosevelt*

I was speaking to a group of parents at a school recently, I do that a lot, and this sweet, sweet mom sheepishly raises her hand with not one but five questions that I welcome joyfully. She kept emphasizing that her children did not yet have smartphones but shared that each of her children under the age of 12 had iPads.

Also, she knew as the words were leaving her mouth what my response was going to be as she admitted, "And I don't have the password to my son's iPad. And he won't give it to me."

My heart went out to her, and I also simultaneously wanted to shake her because I've been there. I get it, but it's also completely unacceptable. We should have our kids' passwords, because passwords are doorways.

We should stop letting tech rule our households and come up with meaningful rules to control tech's grip on our lives.

Because you read this book, you will be way more informed, empowered, and equipped with data to avoid the mistakes that parents like me have made for the past two decades.

Thank you for caring enough to read this.

I wish you well in your parenting journey as you employ the tools and recommendations in this book. I'm sure that with dedication and awareness you can guide your children to adulthood and know that I (and the entire Parenting in a Tech World community) are cheering you on.

Notes

1. Hedderson, M.M. et al. (2023). Trends in screen time use among children during the COVID-19 pandemic, July 2019 through August 2021. *JAMA Network Open*. https://www.ncbi.nlm.nih.gov/pmc/articles/PMC9932850/#:~:text=Conclusions%20and%20Relevance-,These%20findings%20suggest%20that%20screen%20time%20among%20children%20increased%20during,health%20needs%20to%20be%20determined.
2. Attorney General Schwalb Sues TikTok for Preying on District Children, Operating an Illegal Virtual Economy. https://oag.dc.gov/release/attorney-general-schwalb-sues-tiktok-preying.

10

Q (and More Importantly, A)

If you were to attend one of my speaking engagements, chances are you would hear at least one, if not many, of these questions during the question-and-answer portion of the event. Since I can't be all the places all the time and since you took the time to purchase and read this book (thank you), I figured I'd populate the top questions parents have for me no matter where I go.

My child is an artist/athlete and posts their creations/performances on YouTube/Instagram/TikTok—how can I keep them safe?

Social media is a blessing and a curse. It's a blessing that your child's work, performance, or creation could reach so many people so quickly. It's also a curse if their content is used against them (bullying) or provides a portal for predators to communicate with them. That said, you have options. Given that college recruiters will frequently scan social media profiles to assess accepting future students, I would advise that *you*, the parent, manage the child's "portfolio" account. Now, I don't say this lightly. I realize that the last thing you need is one more thing on your plate to manage. However, you can use this as an opportunity to collaborate with your child to curate a responsible digital footprint with them. And if/when DMs come in, make sure you review them together.

My child is an athlete and has been told that a social media profile is a critical component of college recruitment. How can I keep them safe?

Same answer as above.

My child is the only one in (5th, 6th, 7th, 8th) grade without a smartphone and is begging for one. When is the right age to give a child a smartphone?

First of all, let us take a minute to celebrate this wise choice you've made as their parent to do what's best for them and not cave to the pressures that so many other parents have. I'd do some digging to see if, in fact, your child is truly the only one. That can be accomplished a variety of ways, including making a post asking in the grade-level Facebook group (if your child's school has one) just asking if any other parents have delayed giving access. You will be surprised to see who chimes in and what they say. You are most likely not alone. That said, the "right" time to give a child a smartphone truly depends on a few variables:

- *Time Spent Alone*

  If your child is never really alone, reflect honestly on if they actually need a phone at this moment in time. If they are always with a safe adult who already has a smartphone—either parent, teacher, coach, or babysitter—chances are they probably don't. Now, flipside, if the child has to wait solo while you carpool other kids around or perhaps has to spend time with an adult that is less than trustworthy, then it sounds like they could benefit from having a connected mobile device in case of emergency.

- *What Kind of Smartphone*

  Not all smartphones are created equal. Giving your child an iPhone—either hand-me-down or brand new—is like giving them a Lamborghini for their first car. While exciting, sleek, and beautiful, it's not a good choice. It allows them to go from 0 to 60 MPH with minimal protections (think a malfunctioning seat belt in the Lambo) and little oversight (think no car insurance).

  I know that sounds like a dramatic stretch, and I know that many of you reading this have already done so—but please don't throw this book in the fireplace. I'm not judging you. I made that same mistake—I let my son have an iPhone way before I should have—so

I'm giving you this advice not only as an executive at a tech company that helps to protect close to 7 million children across the nation but also as a mom who has been there, done that, and wishes she didn't. If and when it is time for your child to have the ability to text or call or video chat with trusted contacts, and you'd like to be able to keep tabs on their location, and maybe even eventually access certain apps or games, please pick a safer smartphone for their first smartphone.

It doesn't have to be the Bark Phone. There are a few decent choices out there. None offers the comprehensive level of monitoring we do, but almost any smartphone, dumb phone, or flip phone is better than handing a kid an iPhone. And yes, I mean even with setting up Apple's built-in "parental controls" through their Family Center. Apple's parental controls are notoriously buggy, confusing, constantly changing, and don't prioritize child safety. Apple prioritizes complete privacy, which is great for adults, not so much for children who need guidance. As my brilliant colleague Haley Zapal states, "The Internet wasn't built for kids. The Bark Phone was." She's good. Did I mention she's also a lawyer and *Jeopardy* champion? But she uses her time and talents for our mission at Bark, and we are so very thankful for her and even put that line on our very first billboard in the great state of Texas.

- *Their Maturity Level*

  Do they lose things easily (I mean, I still do in my 40s, but you know what I mean)? Do they have at least one good friend or a solid group of friends or teammates? Can they handle little bouts of independence and responsibility? All things to consider.

- *Their Mental Health*

  If your child struggles in any way, shape, or form with anxiety, depression, or is neurodivergent (ADHD, ASD, Asperger's, etc.), you will need to pay close attention to the time they spend connected as it can negatively impact their mood, health, grades, sleep, and interpersonal relationships.

- *What Conversations You've Had*

  Before you let your child have access—even filtered and monitored access—it's important that you've had age-appropriate conversations with them about all of the tough topics including but not limited to mental health, physical health (i.e. screen time impacting physical movement), sexual content/pornography, violent content, drug- and alcohol-related content, predation, disclosure of personally identifiable information, bullying, digital footprints, and more. If you need help with how to have age-appropriate conversations about these topics, please don't hesitate to reach out to your child's pediatrician or school counselor and of course you can flip to Chapter 12 for an extensive list of resources.

My child says Snapchat is the only way kids communicate these days and they will be left out if they don't have it. What should I do? Is Snapchat really that bad?
Snapchat really is that bad. I'll start there.
That said, let's level set about what they will actually be left out of:

- Bullying
- Toxic grade-level group chats (what on Earth could go wrong with 100 6th graders in an app meant for disappearing nudes?)
- Sexual content
- Drug deals
- Comparison trap
- Fear of missing out
- Live location-sharing with potential strangers
- Predation
- Misinformation from AI built right into the app

My advice, from both a personal and professional lens, is to wait as long as possible to let them have access, and certainly not before the age of 16.

I don't have the password for my child's device/account. What should I do?
Um, get it. ASAP. And if they won't give it to you, they lose access. Period. Even if that means you have to call the phone company and disable their phone line—just know you have that card to play. Please do not be afraid to be their parent—both in real life and online. They need you. There's a reason they don't live on their own yet with only one key to their place. The same logic applies to their digital spaces. Now, flipside, should you be an overbearing helicopter parent and abuse that access? No. Please don't.

Whenever we have friends over they bring their devices. What should I do?

Take them away (gently) by placing them in a basket in a common area (like the kitchen) so if they need to text mom or dad they can, but—from the basket. We don't take the devices out of the basket in this house, and we don't move the basket to another room.

I've heard sleepovers are a bad idea in general. Do you agree?

Yes. And I know that is hard to hear, but if you have ever been to a sleepover, you know that rules are different, sometimes more relaxed, and your kids are exposed to risky situations in many cases. And that was back in the day. The worst things we could experience were frozen underwear, lack of sleep, a *Playboy* magazine, and perhaps someone's creepy dad or inappropriate older brother (which is heartbreaking if you or your loved ones experienced abuse in real life at a sleepover, and I am not minimizing that in any way, shape, or form). Enter screens, social media, and the Internet—and all of those risks are now amplified. As my friend and colleague Chris McKenna of Protect Young Eyes says in the powerful documentary *Childhood 2.0*, "Because what they see, they feel neurologically compelled to do." There are certain behaviors you don't want explored or reenacted at a sleepover, including graphic, violent, pornographic situations that kids may have seen on their unfiltered Internet or mobile devices. You also don't want the time kids spend together being silly, sharing their deep thoughts and feelings captured on someone's smartphone or iPad, only to be abused and distributed later in a cyberbullying or sexting situation. Alternatively, you can decide that if a sleepover is going to happen, it's going to happen at *your* house. Also, if children are going to bring connected tech with them to your house, that tech gets to stay in a basket in the kitchen and not wander behind closed doors. You can also do a sleep *under*—and enjoy all the fun parts of getting together (popcorn, movies, pajamas, games, stories, sleeping bags, tents, etc.), but when it's actually time for sleep or unsupervised time, that's when everyone gets picked up (perhaps a little later than normal to make it "fun") to do that *at their own home*.

My kid gets so mad at me—like unreasonably mad at me—when it's time for screen time to end. How can I de-escalate this ongoing struggle?

Imagine someone gave you a huge container of your favorite ice cream and a spoon, and just as you were about to have your first bite, they just took it away. You'd be livid, right?! It's not their fault. It's their brain. Try setting a kitchen timer so they can hear the tick tick tick of the impeding screen time limit and hold firm. Stand your ground. Do not bend or break. You can also work with them (not in that moment but during other peaceful moments like car rides) to educate them on the power that screens and games and shows have on our brain, due to the dopamine spikes taking place. Please see the resources listed in Chapter 12 for more on that.

At what age should I begin talking to my child about pornography?
As soon as they have unmonitored time with a screen that can access the Internet. Two great resources for helping you have this conversation in an age-appropriate way are *Good Pictures Bad Pictures* (ages 7–12) and *Good Pictures Bad Pictures, Jr.* (ages 3–6).

Is there a way to add parental controls to the connected devices in my home?
Yes! So many yeses here. One of the best things you can do as a parent in a tech world is to take a long, hard look at all of the connected tech that your children can access, whether it's "their" device or not—and then head to Google or Parenting in a Tech World (the Facebook Group) or Protect Young Eyes, and type in the name of the device, app, or game (example **Nintendo Switch**) plus two words: **parental controls**.
So, your search would essentially look like this:
"Nintendo switch parental controls"
If you did that, you would stumble upon this handy link: www.nintendo.com/us/switch/parental-controls and realize that there is an app for this! Meaning, Nintendo has a parental control app live in the app store (both Apple and Google Play) meant to help parents manage their child's Nintendo Switch device!
Now, how many parents do you think actually know about this app? Not many. And how many parents do you know have taken advantage of this app? Probably even less than that.
Backing up to the original question, though—there is a way to add parental controls to connected devices; it's a layered approach and it's not quick, but it's very, very important.

My recommendation is to take the following steps, in this order:

1. Figure out who your home **Internet service provider** is, log in to your account on their portal, download their app, or call/email customer service and implement the *free* parental controls that come with your service. For example, I just did this with a local family who uses AT&T. They learned that AT&T offers something called Smart Home Manager, which includes the ability to create profiles (where you can assign devices to users on your Wi-Fi network), set content controls, set time limits for profiles, and pause or restart the Internet for specific devices or profiles. In our home, the Internet is provided by Xfinity, and they have the same thing! Chances are, whoever you use for home Internet service will have some form of baked-in, free parental controls. Please use them.

2. Figure out who your **cellular service provider** is, and just like above, utilize the tools they give you that you are already paying for. For example, T-Mobile offers apps and services like Family-Mode, Safe & Found, Family Allowances, FamilyWhere, and Web Guard to help manage all that comes with your family's mobile devices. Is that a lot to sort through and decipher? Sure. Is it worth it? Yep. Verizon has its own set of offerings (not free), as does AT&T Wireless with their AT&T Secure Family offering, separate from their Internet service mentioned in the first point above.

3. Figure out **what tech you have in your house that can connect to the Internet,** either via the Internet or cellular service just mentioned above. This includes smart TVs and gaming consoles, not just smartphones and tablets.

4. Take a second pass at thinking about what tech you might have lying around in a junk drawer, attic or basement, giveaway bag, or recycle pile. Cracked iPhones, old laptops, ancient Kindles—all of that tech can be powered on and become an access point—so might be time to do some donating/recycling or…protecting!

5. Then, as you can probably guess by now, it's time to **head to "the google"** (that's a tech joke, it just means Google it) and search for the name of the thing plus *parental controls*. For example:

   - Samsung Smart TV Parental Controls
   - Roku Parental Controls
   - Alexa Parental Controls
   - Xbox Parental Controls
   - iPhone Parental Controls
   - PS5 Parental Controls
   - Netflix Parental Controls
   - Kindle Parental Controls

   and then, follow the (ideally) clear instructions on how to implement the various tools and settings.

   Yes, across *all* of those devices, every single one.

6. Are we done yet? Are we there yet? Nope. Next we need to dig further into each of those devices once we've applied blanket controls, filters, and time limits and implement app- and game-specific parental controls.

   For example, chances are your smart TV has a slew of apps that are perfectly acceptable for an adult to access. In some cases, you have the ability to set PINs to block access to those apps if you don't want your child accessing them—or the ability to just delete them altogether.

   I was recently at a family's house that had a Samsung Smart TV. When we went to Settings ➤ Apps, guess which was the first on the list?

   It wasn't Netflix, HBO, Hulu, or even ESPN.

   It was freaking TikTok.

   They were shook. (Er, that's another way of saying shocked.)

   That's where we are, people. And the onus is on us to be hypervigilant in the tech space until things change on the legislative front.

7. Finally, location is key. If you can keep connected tech out of bedrooms at night, that's more than half the battle. Think about doing that for yourselves as well. I guarantee you will sleep better.

8. Can't someone make this easier for parents? Yes—we've tried that at Bark, and while it's still complicated because you are dealing with

so many variables with devices and service providers, we offer the Bark Home (for the connected tech in your home), Bark Smartphone (the safest yet coolest smartphone for kids with the most advanced content monitoring on the planet—I'm not exaggerating—because no other company has been working on a unique data set like ours for as long as we have), Bark Smart Watch (much safer than an Apple Watch but still super sleek), and, finally, Bark App that you manage all from *one* single dashboard on your phone or computer. You can learn more and see if Bark is right for your family at https://bark.us.

My kids don't have smartphones but they have iPads. What do I need to know?

You can do all the things on an iPad that you can do on a smartphone as long as that iPad has some sort of connectivity—either Wi-Fi or LTE (cell signal). So essentially, they already have a smartphone of sorts. Please take the time to implement the built-in parental controls that Apple offers (covered earlier in this chapter), please only allow your children to use the iPad in open areas of the home and not in bedrooms or bathrooms, and please consider connecting the iPad to Bark's monitoring service. You'd be blown away by what our algorithm has uncovered for parents just like you and how it has helped them gain critical insights into their child's unique world of peers and interests.

My children love *Roblox*. Is it really that dangerous?

It can be. It absolutely can be. According to a local Atlanta Internet Crimes Against Children (ICAC) officer, *Roblox* was the most concerning platform when it came to kids and predation over the past two years. There are a variety of factors that go into that assessment—but knowing that Roblox is the most popular platform for children ages 5–12, and, "in the first quarter of 2024, gaming company Roblox Corporation had over 32 million daily active users of Roblox games under the age of 13."[1] certainly makes it an attractive place for predators to spend time as well.[2]

Now to be fair to *Roblox*, the people working on their Trust and Safety team have implemented parental controls and settings to make it harder for children to be bullied, exploited, and abused on their platform. Please do not let your children play this game without **turning on those free features** and

reviewing (together-amazing learning experience) **helpful tools** like how to block, report, or mute a user who is acting creepy or unkind.

Why do you say iPhones are bad for kids and Androids are better? Doesn't Apple offer parental controls and location tracking?

Apple prioritizes privacy, not child safety. The two cannot coexist in the current Apple ecosystem. That's why we had to literally build our very own smartphone with the Bark platform built into it. And that's why we chose Android as our model to do so.

What's the worst app out there?

Snapchat is the worst app for children. The reason this app was created by Evan Spiegel and Bobby Murphy in September 2011 was to send disappearing nudes. It was marketed as "the relaunch of the photo sharing app Picaboo," but it had one main purpose: sexting without a trace. Seems like a great app for kids to have? No? Definitely not.

What are the riskiest apps for kids?

Any apps that allow the child to message another human, write words, share photos, share videos, send voice messages, video chat, surf the unfiltered web, chat with an AI bot, etc. So, basically, all of them.

What are the safest apps for kids?

Apps that don't allow for messaging with unknown contacts, surfing the web (using a browser), have zero advertising, and have built-in time limits.

Is it okay for my child to have a TV or gaming console in their room?

No, it's really not—but please know that I made this mistake, so I get how easy it can be to allow this "gift" into a child's room and how hard it can be to walk that decision back.

How do I know when my child is truly ready for social media?

Short answer: Wait until they are at *least* 16 years of age.

Longer answer: Let me put it like this—at age 15 (in the United States of America, at least) we make kids pass a test before they are able to operate a vehicle (an amazing tool that also has the power to kill, just like social media), and even then, that gives them the ability to do so only under conditions where an adult is present to ride alongside them. For a full year. And then, they have to pass another test to be able to go it alone. Also, car insurance rates are jacked way up until they turn 25ish because insurance companies know that our frontal lobes aren't fully formed until we are in our early to mid-twenties. So if we've decided as a modern society that children aren't ready for life-altering tools until 15 with overt guidance for another year—why in the world are we giving elementary school kids that same power/access in digital form? It's truly ludicrous.

How do I make sure my kids sleep at night instead of sneaking online to game while *we* sleep?

Don't let your kids have connected tech in their bedrooms or behind closed doors. Additionally, because good kids make bad choices especially when addictive technology is involved, and they will inevitably find a way to sneak a connected device into a room with a door that can close during the day or night, you can also set your home ISP to have time limits that apply to all the connected tech in the home or even granular-level settings. Bark Home can help with this as well.

My child is being bullied. What can/should I do?

First, I want to extend my heartfelt sympathies to you, as it hurts so very much to see your child struggling with this issue. I've been there. It's the worst. Next, assess the situation, which—as I completely get—can be very nuanced.

If your child is in grade school and the bully is as well, the first ideal steps would be to reach out to the parents of the bully to see if your families can work through the issues together. Note that I said *ideal*. These situations are hardly ideal. Next, you can reach out to your school's principal/counselor/teacher/coach to bring them up to speed on what's happening and make a game plan for next steps.

It's important to note that if the bullying has a digital component to it, I would strongly suggest you take screen shots to preserve any evidence in case it gets to that point of needing to have proof of the conversations/communications.

Finally, know that you have legal options as well. StopBullying.gov is an incredibly comprehensive and helpful website that walks you through tips and provides an overview of state-by-state bullying laws.

My child is struggling with mental health issues. What should I do?

Please call your child's pediatrician, even if it's after hours or on the weekend.

What are the dangers of TikTok?

Oh boy. You might want to pour a cup of tea and sit down for this one. Not only is the hype about it being an app influenced by the Chinese government a very credible concern (at least if you are a high-ranking government or military official)—as it relates to everyday citizens and children—it's one of the most highly addictive apps I've ever encountered. And remember, I've been engrossed in this world since it was born. The algorithms are so powerful that they can turn a sad child into a majorly depressed child. They can turn a self-conscious child into one who starts to struggle with an eating disorder. TikTok is responsible for so much misinformation it's terrifying. Outside of the pure fact that it's keeping children from physically moving their bodies and interacting with other humans, their parents, siblings, and peers in real life, it's exacerbating mental health issues, preventing sleep, and honestly contributing to the mass dumbing down of American kids. There is a reason that the TikTok feed in China is only educational content with built-in time limits.[3]

I'm not ready for my kid to have a smartphone. What do you think about smart watches?

Smart watches are a great way for kids to have limited connectivity and location tracking while mitigating the harms that come with unsafe smartphones as well as the loss/theft factor. While not completely foolproof in terms of exposure to harmful content and people (if you've chosen to go with an Apple watch), there are safer smart watch alternatives out there like Gizmo and Gabb, and of course, my first choice is the Bark Watch. I know and highly respect the engineering team that worked on this, and it is the best option on the market.

Smart watches are better than smartphones for younger kids who lose things easily and don't need all the functions of a smartphone.

Is there a way to make YouTube safer for my kids? What about YouTube kids?

This is complicated but doable. The problem lies in the fact that unlike other social media platforms (yes, YouTube is absolutely social media) YouTube videos are able to be accessed across all browsers without having to log in to a profile.

So you can go through the motions of turning on safe search etc., but at the end of the day, it's nowhere near failproof.

Outside of blocking the URL, it will continue to be one of the technological banes of our existence as parents.

Why are group text chats for kids so problematic?

Ask any elementary or middle school principal and they will ask you how much time you have because, boy, they could tell you some stories.

It's the worst of peer pressure, amplified, and desensitized because every kid is behind a screen and not face-to-face, having to deal with raw emotion and the ramifications of their typed words.

Should phones be allowed in school?

No and yes. I firmly believe that if it's a safer smartphone with time limits, filters, and monitoring (so, the Bark Phone) and it's kept out of sight, then it's fine for kids to have that tech in case of emergency.

One major argument *for* allowing phones in schools is due to the unfortunate frequency of school shooting violence in the United States. I will say, even with that looming and credible threat, it's way more critical for kids to not be distracted by mom or dad texting them during a crisis and instead focused on staying silent, calm, following instructions, and getting to safety. So what I'm saying is that, as a mom, I absolutely want to be able to text my son 24/7/365, but as a rational adult removing emotion from the situation, I realize it's better for my son and everyone else if that phone stays away during the school day. Yes, for the entire school day, even lunch, recess, bathroom breaks, etc.

Until science shows that digital learning is better for kids than physical paper and pen, and shows that kids thrive with tiny supercomputers in their pockets during elementary and middle school, I'll stand firm on this hill.

Is there a way to safely share photos and videos of my kids online?

Let's first start with storing photos/video since the average child will have more than 2,000 digital photos captured of them before the age of two years old.

Dropbox, iCloud, Amazon, Google Drive—anything with two-factor authentication (2FA) and a strong password—are great places for storing media. In terms of sharing, I'd really caution you against sharing too much with too many people, period.

Please make sure your privacy settings are actually set (meaning, don't share photos and videos of your children on public profiles) and refrain from sharing any bathtub, bathing suit, or leotard photos/videos as much as possible.

I know it's hard to hear that some of the people in your close circle of contacts could do and think bad things with your child's content, but ask anyone in law enforcement or child safety and they will confirm—it's just better if you don't.

My child has been contacted by an online predator. What should I do?

It depends on what else has happened. If your child has not engaged in any conversations or sent any photos or videos, then please take screenshots to document all possible evidence, then block, then report to law enforcement. Let law enforcement work on the nuance of reporting to the platform so that the predator doesn't get tipped off too soon.

If your child has engaged in lengthy conversations or sent media (or personally identifiable information), it probably warrants a trip to your pediatrician or child mental healthcare professional to assess next steps. The ICAC units across the United States have victim advocates who are well-trained in helping children through this nuanced situation.

My child sent/received a nude photo/video. What should I do?

If sent to a peer, please reach out and ask them to delete due to potential legal ramifications.

If sent to a stranger, please reach out to NCMEC's Take It Down or your local law enforcement.

If received, have your child delete it immediately.

How much screen time is too much (really)?

That depends on the age and stage of the child. Please consult with your pediatrician, and please delay as much as possible especially during the birth to age five stage. When in doubt, default to less than two hours of screen time per day. That is a gross generalization, but this is the Q&A section, not a research thesis. According to the American Academy of Pediatrics, "Because children and adolescents can have many different kinds of interactions with technology, rather than setting a guideline for specific time limits on digital media use, we recommend considering the quality of interactions with digital media and not just the quantity, or amount of time."[4]

How do I know if my kids are safe on their school-issued tech?

You won't know until you ask. Don't be afraid to ask your school's administration (principal, guidance counselor, IT director, librarian, or teacher) what tech your child can access while on campus, how they are making sure it's as safe as possible, and what holes exist in that plan. Make sure to also ask how you are expected to keep that tech experience safe for them in the event they are asked to take those devices home.

How can I get other parents to care as much as I do about these issues?

Show them *Childhood 2.0*. Share the *Scrolling2Death* podcast with them. Share social media posts and videos by Protect Young Eyes and Bark Technologies, and, well, me—if you'd like.

Help me understand AI and all this ChatGPT stuff.

Here's the deal. AI stands for artificial intelligence. It's an incredible advancement for us as humans when it comes to computer science, but it's also really freaking scary if used unethically. We won't focus on that in this book, though. If you like analogies, it's like the day people figured out how to use calculators and no longer had to use their brains, fingers, or pencil and paper to do math. But amplify that by 1 million. So how does it relate to you and your kids? Well, AI is rapidly being integrated into every aspect of our lives. It's hard to escape these days, and I suggest you sit down with your child and learn from them and with them. More resources on understanding AI are provided in Chapter 12.

Notes

1. Statista (2024). Daily active users (DAU) of Roblox games worldwide from 4th quarter 2019 to 2nd quarter 2024, by age group. https://www .statista.com/statistics/1190309/daily-active-users-worldwide-roblox/#:~:text=Roblox%20games%20global%20DAU%20as%20 of%20Q1%202024%2C%20by%20age%20group&text=In%20the%20 first%20quarter%20of,in%20the%20same%20age%20group
2. Statista (2024). Daily active users (DAU) of Roblox games worldwide from 4th quarter 2019 to 2nd quarter 2024, by age group. https://www .statista.com/statistics/1190309/daily-active-users-worldwide-roblox/#:~:text=Roblox%20games%20global%20DAU%20as%20

of%20Q1%202024%2C%20by%20age%20group&text=In%20the%20
first%20quarter%20of,in%20the%20same%20age%20group

3. Yang, Z. (2023). How China takes extreme measures to keep teens off TikTok. *Technology Review*. https://www.technologyreview.com/2023/ 03/08/1069527/china-tiktok-douyin-teens-privacy/.

4. American Academy of Pediatrics (2023). Screen time guidelines. https:// www.aap.org/en/patient-care/media-and-children/center-of- excellence-on-social-media-and-youth-mental-health/qa-portal/ qa-portal-library/qa-portal-library-questions/screen-time-guidelines/ ?srsltid=AfmBOorWc0N2E_nXg3l8pArgxa-v9DgHCHtrKdZ9BnZX eL8P52ehn5Pt.

11

Glossary, Emoji, Acronym Translator

Every generation has had their own jargon, slang, iconography, pictographs, and brands that become a household name. Think the smiley face from the 60s, Kleenex, and Kool-Aid from the past. Or today, Google, "bro," LOL, or the laughing crying emoji. Acronyms and initialisms have served us as well. The ability to shorten a longer phrase by simply using the first letter, or initial, to make a new word makes sense for a culture so pressed for time. It's fitting how the Information Age has had such an explosion of new terms, acronyms, and emoji. And did you know that the word "emoji" comes from the Japanese words e ("picture") and moji ("character")? Because I did *not* until I started writing this chapter.

This glossary, emoji, and acronym translator is all courtesy of, and thanks to, the years of dedicated data science work and research from the team at Bark Technologies combined with in-the-field conversations with families across the globe. Get ready to get familiar.

There are so many here that are eye-opening, and one that I think a lot of people are surprised by is the pasta noodle emoji. You might see this 🍜 if you are scanning through your child's communications and think, "Cool, no big deal, so my kid is interested in having Italian food for dinner."

Sure, could be. Or—noodles sound like nudes. And so there you go.

If you see the pasta noodle emoji on your child's digital communications and you're not having Italian for dinner, it might be something you want to take a second look at.

These next few pages will contain surprises like that, some you may have heard of and some that potentially neither you nor your child will ever use seriously.

*420 Marijuana reference.

*11:11 Popular time to make a wish.

AF As f**k.

AFK Stands for "away from keyboard" and is used when a player steps away, like "BRB."

A mood A relatable feeling or situation (often shortened to the single word, "mood").

And that's on [*something*] Used to indicate that you've just shared a truth that needs no further discussion.

*ASB As balls. Example: I'm high asb.

ASL Age/sex/location.

Ate/Ate that Means you successfully did something; you pulled it off. Example: "I saw your prom pics on insta, you totally ate that look." If someone "ate that"—they did it well, unlike in our generation which meant someone took a nasty fall. See also: "Left no crumbs."

Avatar What a player's character looks like in the game. You can customize them with features, props, and clothes, and more. This is kind of like a Bitmoji (your own personal emoji).

Bae Often a pet name for a significant other or crush. Short for "baby."

Basic Someone who is viewed as boring or a conforming person.

Beige flag A quality or characteristic of a significant other that is weird or off-putting, but not enough to reject them.

Benching Just like in sports, benching someone in dating means putting them to the side to date other people. Benching is usually brought on when they do something to annoy or upset you.

Bet A response indicating agreement. Example: "Wanna go to the store?" "Bet."

Bestie "Best friend"; can also be used as a kind of formal address to a stranger.

Bih   Short form of b★tch.

Body count   The number of people someone has slept with.

Boss   The final bad guy a player has to beat in every level. They're usually bigger, stronger, and harder to beat than the others.

Breadcrumbing   When someone leads you on by flirting and making you feel special but without any intention to actually commit to a relationship. What's left is a "breadcrumb" trail that keeps you attached.

Bruh   "Bro"; can be used to address anybody.

BTS   A Korean boy band popular with tweens and teens.

Bussin'   Awesome. Example: These tacos are bussin'.

Cake   Used to describe a large bottom.

Camping   When a character stays in one spot—"camps out"—to gain an unfair advantage and attack other characters without being seen.

Canon event   A moment in development that will help shape your life or personality.

Cappin'   Lying.

Cart   Cartridge for a vaporizer.

CEO of [something]   To be a representative of some activity or thing. Example: "Taylor is the CEO of sleeping in late."

★Chad   A hyper-sexual young man.

Cheugy   Used to describe someone or something that is basic, out of date, or trying too hard.

COD   Short for *Call of Duty*, one of the most popular first-person shooter video games in history.

★Coney   Slang for "penis."

Crafting   The act of building virtual items in a game. For example, collecting rubbing alcohol and cloth to make a first-aid kit.

Cuffing/Cuffing season   "Cuffing" simply means to get into a relationship. "Cuffing season" specifically refers to winter, when you'd want someone to snuggle with while it's colder outside.

Cursed   Used to describe something (usually an online image) that is unsettling or creepy.

Cringe   Causing feelings of embarrassment or awkwardness.

CYA   "Cover your ass" or "see ya."

Dabbing   A way to inhale concentrated cannabis oil by dropping some on a hot surface and letting it vaporize, also a dance move that was popular in 2015.

Daddy An attractive man, usually older, who conveys a sense of power and dominance.

Ded Used when something is really funny or embarrassing. Example: That meme has me ded!

Delulu Short for "delusional" and used when someone has unrealistic ideas about something.

DLC Stands for "downloadable content" that gamers can buy for a video game. It ranges from cosmetic upgrades all the way to new levels and game expansions.

Do it for the plot Said to encourage oneself to take a chance on something. Example: I'm going to try out for the basketball team. Even if I don't make it, I'll do it for the plot."

*Dongle Slang for "penis."

Dope A way to describe something as cool or awesome.

DPS Stands for "damage per second" and refers to the amount of destruction a player can exert in a single second. The higher the DPS, the more deadly the player.

Drip Style, great fashion sense, flashy accessories.

DTF Down to f*ck.

DTR Stands for "define the relationship." This usually occurs after the "talking phase" (see below) when both parties have expressed feelings and it's time to decide if both want to make it official.

Easter egg A hard-to-find image, message, feature, or location hidden in a video game. An example would be a poster on a character's bedroom wall that depicts the video game developer's favorite movie.

Egirl/Eboy A young person with emo-inspired, punk-rock style.

Esports The catchall term for competitive, professional gaming where players (often on leagues or teams) go head-to-head for lots of money.

ESRB Ratings for games.

Facts An emphatic way to acknowledge the truth of someone's statement.

Fam Friends.

FBOI F**k boy; a guy just looking for sex.

FINSTA Fake Instagram account.

Fire Amazing.

FOMO Fear of missing out.

FPS Stands for "first-person shooter"; a type of weapons-based game where the player sees through a character's eyes and interacts with the world head-on.

FWB Friends with benefits.

Gas Can refer to marijuana, be used to describe something that's cool, or be used as a verb to mean "hype someone up."

Gaslighting This has become a popular term on the Internet, but it refers to a form of psychological manipulation in which a significant other makes you feel crazy or wrong, even when unjustified.

GG Stands for "good game"; usually said in the text chat after a game ends.

GG EZ Stands for "good game, easy" and snarkily implies that a player had no challenge in beating their opponent.

Ghosting/Ghosted A term that's been around for quite a while now; ghosting is essentially getting dumped with no explanation. One day you're talking to each other and things seem fine—the next day, radio silence and the relationship is over. People often ghost instead of dumping someone. The youth of today (and some adults too now) will end a relationship by completely disappearing with no further communication.

Glitching When a player exploits a bug (or glitch) in a video game to get an unfair advantage, like running through walls.

Goals Something you want or aspire to.

GOAT Greatest of all time.

Griefing Intentionally annoying, harassing, or trolling other players in a video game, usually through voice or text chat.

GTG Got to go.

Gucci Something good or cool.

GYAT Kids might tell you it means "get your act together" if you (or a teacher) ask(s)—but it actually references a large shapely bottom, is used to express approval or excitement, or is a shortened term for using the Lord's name in combination with the word damn.

Hentai Graphic anime pornography.

HEAF An acronym for "high expectations Asian father."

High key 1. Very interested in. 2. Actively spreading information.

Hits different   When something is better than it normally is because of different circumstances. Example: "A cold soda just hits different when it's super-hot outside."

Hulk   A 2-mg generic benzodiazepine bar that is green.

Ick or Ick Factor   The feeling you get when your attraction to someone is suddenly flipped to a feeling of disgust. Similar to a red flag, the ick factor is when there's a certain quality or trait about another person that you just simply don't like. It's usually small things, but they can add up to make that person undatable. Some popular examples from the Internet include when guys wear flip-flops or when girls wear too much makeup.

★ILY   I love you.

★IRL   In real life.

ISO   In search of.

IYKYK   "If you know you know"; meant to imply that there's an inside joke.

★JK   Just kidding.

Juul   Type of e-cigarette that is small and discreet; "pods" are used for smoking.

Karen   Used to refer to an entitled older woman.

Killstreak   The total number of consecutive kills a player can rack up before dying themselves.

KMS   Kill myself.

KYS   Kill yourself.

Lag   When there's a delay between a player's action and on-screen activity, similar to when Zoom freezes up during a call.

Left no crumbs   A phrase that means you did something perfectly. Can be used in conjunction with "ate that"—means they did something exceptionally well.

Let him cook   Do not interfere.

Lit/Turnt/Turnt Up   Something that's active or popular can also refer to being stoned or drunk.

LMP   1. A term that means "like my pic." 2. Sometimes stands for "lick my p★★★y."

Lobby   A lobby is a menu screen where players wait before a game officially begins. They can learn about the next game session, look at results from the last, change settings, and talk to each other. In many games, players return to the lobby after each session. Think of it like a waiting room.

Loot The beneficial items a player can pick up while playing, usually after killing an enemy. Ammo and health are common examples of loot that players can scavenge.

Loot boxes An example of "pay to win" gaming, where players use real money to get randomized "loot boxes" that may contain skins, weapons, and in-game advantages. This system has come under criticism for being a little too much like gambling.

Low key 1. Somewhat interested in. 2. Keeping information secret.

Matchmaking The process by which a game assigns players against each other, usually taking into account skill level and ranking.

Meal Someone who looks good enough to eat. See also: "Snack" or "snack."

Mewing The act of making your jawline more defined by putting your tongue to the roof of your mouth. Teens might say something like, "Can't talk, mewing" to indicate this is why they're not talking.

Mid Insult meaning "low quality" or "average." Derives from "mid-tier"—not awful, but not great. Example: "The new *Jurassic Park* movie was mid."

MMORPG Stands for "massively multiplayer online role-playing game"; these are usually sci-fi or fantasy games (*World of Warcraft* is a good example) that allow players to interact with large numbers of other players.

Mod Short for "modification"; refers to when a player changes an aspect of the game to create a new feature.

*Netflix and chill Getting together and hooking up.

No Cap Used to indicate that someone is not lying.

Noob Refers to an inexperienced gamer; derived from "newbie."

NPC Stands for "non-player character"; that is, characters controlled by the computer.

OFC Short for "of course."

OK, Boomer Calling out an idea that is outdated or resistant to change.

*OKURRR Variation of "OKAY" made popular by rapper Cardi B who defines it as something that is said to affirm when someone is being put in their place.

OP   Stands for "overpowered," typically in reference to a gun or ammo type in the game.

Opp   Someone you are not on good terms with, like an opponent.

Pen   Vape for weed or tobacco; uses cartridges.

Pink flags   Based on the idea of red flags, pink flags are a step down. They aren't huge warning signals that something is wrong, but they can hint that this relationship isn't super healthy.

Plug   Term used to refer to someone who can "connect" you with drugs; a drug dealer.

Preppy   Used to refer to a particular aesthetic that involves girly, bright-colored clothes and popular name brands, such as Lululemon and Stanley. It's similar to the definition of preppy we grew up with, but slightly more refined and "basic."

PvE   Stands for "player versus environment." This could be a monster that players have to beat, for example.

PvP   Stands for "player versus player."

Pwned   Pronounced "poned" (like moaned), this term is a variation of "owned"—originally from a typo because the letters P and O are next to each other on a computer keyboard. To pwn someone means to have mastery over them. Example: "I beat you three times in a row in *Fortnite*! You totally got pwned!"

Rage Quit   To angrily leave a game in frustration.

Respawn   Refers to when a player comes back to life after being killed in-game.

Rizz   Derived from "charisma." Someone who has "game" when it comes to romantic pursuits. Example: "Taylor has that rizz, they're so charming."

★ROTFLMAO   Rolling on the floor laughing my ass off.

Salty   To be bitter or cranky about something.

Same   "I can relate."

★School Bus   A 2 mg Xanax bar, which is yellow.

Scrub   An insult used to demoralize another player, implying that they're bad.

★SH   Sh★★ happens.

Shading   Where teens gossip about another party without naming them; also "throw shade" means to talk about someone.

Ship   Short for "relationship"; also used as a verb to indicate a desire to see two people together. Example: I ship Taylor and Jamie.

Sigma   Someone who is a lone-wolf type, quiet, independent but still strong. As opposed to the more dominant "Alpha" male type.

Simp   Somebody who tries very hard (a.k.a. a "try-hard") and does a lot for their crush or significant other. Example: "You got Sarah 3 dozen roses? Stop being such a simp."

Sis   Short for "sister" but can be used to address anybody; usually used to express that drama has occurred.

Situationship   Describes two people who are not officially dating but who have feelings for each other.

Skeet   To ejaculate.

Skibidi toilet   A surreal animated video featuring a singing toilet. It's not supposed to make sense or any sense; it's just a funny video popular with Gen Alpha.

Skins   Term used to describe new avatar customizations that players can buy or collect.

Slaps   Used to express that something is awesome. Example: "This burrito slaps."

Smash   Means to have casual sex.

SMDH   Shaking my damn head.

SMH   "Shaking my head," meaning "I don't believe it" or "that's so dumb."

Snack   Describes an attractive person; someone who looks good enough to eat. Sometimes spelled "snacc."

*Snapstreak   Created when friends send snaps every day, creating a streak.

Snatched   On point, very good, or well styled.

Sneaky link   Refers to someone you're seeing or hooking up with secretly.

Snow   Cocaine.

Spam   A fake social media account.

Special K   Ketamine.

Squeaker   Insult typically used to describe younger gamers (because their voices aren't deep). Note: This is generally used to make fun of male players, but there are—of course—plenty of other types of players with a range of different voices.

Squad   Close friend group.

Stan   A teen slang term meaning an overzealous or obsessive fan of a particular celebrity.

STFU　Short for "shut the f★★k up," can be used as an expression of disbelief or to cyberbully.

Sus　Short for "suspicious." Popularized by the *Among Us* game.

Sweat　Term that describes a try-hard gamer, i.e. someone who goes out of their way to win in an over-the-top, unnecessary way.

Swoop　To be picked up in an automobile.

Talking/Talking phase　This term describes the phase between flirting and official dating. This means you're probably texting this person more than other people in your life but you're nowhere near ready to be exclusive. For example, it's common to hear "No, I'm not dating anyone. But me and this guy from another school are talking."

TBH　To be honest.

Tea　Gossip or interesting news shared between friends.

★TDTM　Talk dirty to me.

Thicc　Having an attractive, curvy body.

TF　The f★★k, as in "who TF do you think you are?"

Thirsty　Desperate for attention, usually sexual or romantic attention.

Thot　Stands for "that ho over there" and is often used instead of "slut."

Trap phone　Also called a burner phone, this is an older, hand-me-down smartphone that kids trade or sell with each other. Kids who get their phones taken away by their parents may seek out a trap phone to have easy Internet access (provided they can connect it to Wi-Fi).

Trash　Terrible or unacceptable.

Twitch　A popular video-game streaming platform. On it, popular gamers play video games live while providing commentary and chatting with fans.

V　"Very."

Vibing　Chilling out, having a good time, or identifying with a certain kind of energy.

★VSCO girl　A style characterized by Hydro Flasks, Crocs, and scrunchies.

WAP　Wet a★★ p★★★y (from the popular Cardi B song released in 2020).

★WTF　What the f★★k?

★WYA　Where you at?

★WYD　What you doing?

★WYF　Where you from?

Woke　Socially or politically conscious.

Wrekd/Wrecked Defeated. This is often used in the expressed "get wrekd."

XP This gaming term stands for "experience points"; they're used to measure your progress through a game. The higher your XP, the more experience you have and the more powers you'll unlock.

YAAS A Very emphatic yes.

Yayo Cocaine.

YEET 1. A very strong word for yes. 2. To throw something.

You a bot A gaming phrase used when someone is acting dumb or playing poorly in a game. Refers to AI bots being easy or bad in games, making it obvious it's not actually a human playing.

Zaddy A well-dressed, attractive man of any age.

Zaza or za Marijuana.

Zombie-ing This happens after someone ghosts you and then decides to start talking to you again like nothing ever happened. A "coming back from the dead," if you will.

★Older but still used

And as if letter and text-based acronyms weren't enough to decipher, let's now look at all the Emoji:

Penis

Used to express drunkenness, sexual arousal, or a grimace

Butt

Means "hot" in a sexual sense; a kid might comment this on their crush's Instagram selfie, for example

 "Dump truck," which refers to a large and/or shapely bottom

Vagina

Used to express annoyance about something

Used when getting caught in a mistake or when feeling like a fraud

Indicates being "ghosted" (dumped with no explanation)

Symbolizes a lie, which could also be called a "cap"

Shy, nervous (usually in the context of flirting)

Represents warding off the "evil eye"

Oral sex

Ejaculation

May indicate sexual activity, especially oral sex

Used when someone has an "hourglass" body shape

Often used in response to a snarky or "savage" comment (as in, "That was cold")

Feeling frisky or naughty

A response that means "It is what it is"

Can be used in comments to denote a sarcastic, mean-spirited tone

Emoji slang for marijuana/weed

Desiring someone sexually (often used in response to nudes)

Breasts/testicles/virginity

Represents nudes, which are often called "noods"

Used when sending or receiving nudes

Often used on TikTok to express wanting something portrayed in the video

A stamp of approval; "I agree"

Used to refer to sexual activity

Indicates "spiciness," i.e. inappropriate or risqué content

Represents "porn," especially on TikTok

I'm literally dead from how powerful that comment was

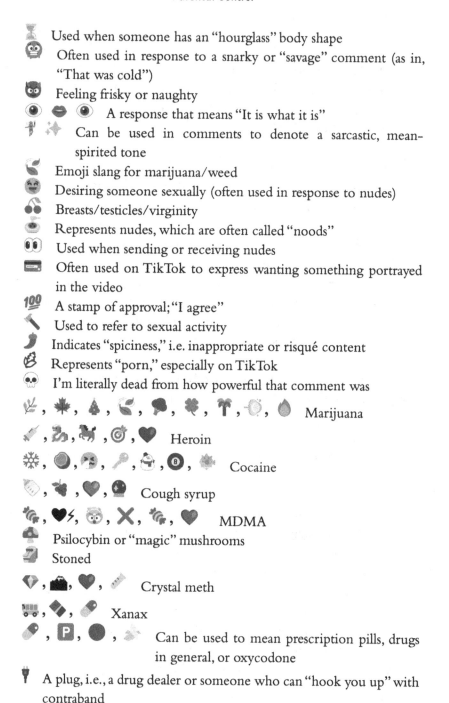

, , , , , , , , Marijuana

, , , , Heroin

, , , , , , Cocaine

, , , Cough syrup

, , , , , MDMA

Psilocybin or "magic" mushrooms

Stoned

, , , Crystal meth

, , Xanax

, , , Can be used to mean prescription pills, drugs in general, or oxycodone

A plug, i.e., a drug dealer or someone who can "hook you up" with contraband

, , ,   Drug deal advertising

,   Smoking a joint

    Used to indicate a bong

    Can mean high-quality or being very intoxicated

    Gassed, i.e., intoxicated; can also refer to high-quality marijuana

    To "blaze" a joint or to be "lit," meaning intoxicated

,   A large amount of drugs

12 | Resources

If the only reason that you purchased or picked up this book was to go over the resources, awesome! You're in the right place. I hope these help you, and if you have any questions or need any support, you can contact me directly via:

titaniajordan.com ∞

General Resources

- *Childhood 2.0* **Documentary:** childhood2movie.com 🎞
- **Bark's Annual Report:** bark.us/annual-report 📎
- **Sexting Laws:** bark.us/blog/state-by-state-differences-in-sexting-laws ⚖
- **Comprehensive and Up-to-Date Slang Guides:** bark.us/blog/teen-text-speak-codes-every-parent-should-know 🍓
- **Parenting in a Tech World, the Facebook Group with more than half a million supportive parents just like you:** facebook.com/groups/parentinggeeks 🚀
- **Family Tech Contract:** bark.us/blog/tech-accountability-create-technology-contract-family 📝
- **Protect Young Eyes:** protectyoungeyes.com 👀
- **Good Pictures, Bad Pictures (a version for kids ages 3–6 and another for older kids ages 7–12):** defendyoungminds.com/books 🔍

- **NCMEC's Take It Down service:** takeitdown.ncmec.org ⃠
- **Internet Crimes Against Children Units:** icactaskforce.org 🔔
- **Cyberbullying Laws:** cyberbullying.org/bullying-laws ⚖️
- **Scrolling2Death Podcast:** scrolling2death.com 🎙️
- **Wait Until 8th:** waituntil8th.org 🤚
- **Children and Screens: Institute for Digital Media and Child Development:** childrenandscreens.org 📺
- **In-Depth Tech Guides/App Reviews:** bark.us/learn/resources 💡
- **DopaMind (tools to help young people navigate tech in the digital age):** dopamindkids.org 💬

Screen Time Management and Internet Filtering Tools
- **Apple:** support.apple.com/en-us/105121
- **Google:** families.google/familylink
- **Bark App (the only one that offers advanced content monitoring with alerts):** bark.us ⏳
- **Bark Home:** bark.us/bark-home 💜

Safer Tech Options
- **Bark Phone:** bark.us/bark-phone 📱
- **Bark Watch:** bark.us/bark-watch ⌚

When it's time to get your child their first or a new smartphone, please consider the Bark Smartphone, a safer smartphone for children and teens. And if you are going to start by introducing your child to a smart watch as their first mobile tech, please consider the Bark Watch.

If you decide not to go with Bark's offerings, please pick any other phone *besides* an iPhone and please choose any other watch besides an Apple Watch. (For a reminder on why iPhones are not the best option for children, please refer to Chapter 8, "Solutions: So What Do We Do?")

There are more and more options coming to market each month as we learn how harmful tech (that is designed for adults) can be for children, and feel free to ask the Parenting in a Tech World Facebook Group specifics that help you decide what's best for your family.

Also, I offer a weekly update via email covering what you need to know to effectively parent in a tech world, and if you respond to it, your response lands in my inbox!

So, feel free to join (it's free) by scanning this QR code:

To contact, connect with, or book me to speak to your community, visit: TitaniaJordan.com 👋

Acknowledgments

First, in every single thing I do, I want to always thank God for giving me life and opening doors where I only see walls. This life is fleeting and temporary. Make it count.

Next, I could not have brought this book from scattered ramblings to a place that flowed without the guidance of Nick Gebhardt. I am so incredibly grateful for his talent, wisdom, patience, empathy, and creative direction.

A special thanks to my mom, dad, sister, husband, in-laws, and best friends—all contributing special excerpts that I may or may not have included (like the idea for a chapter called "Forts, forts, and more forts") but sincerely appreciated as they encouraged me to just keep writing.

Thanks to my one and only son, Jackson. My dear, sweet, smart, beautiful, brilliant son—you might not understand the depths of my love for you until you have a child of your own, and I look forward to that day. I think we will both have a lot of "aha" moments in the future—and hopefully that future for your children and grandchildren will be a safer one based on the work that my team at Bark and countless others are doing today.

Thank you to Brian Bason; Brandon Hilkert; Sam Lo Smith; James Gillespie; Dr. James Andrews; Doug Curling; Trent Scovell; Adina Kalish; Justin Hackney; Jodie Sherrill; Caroline Scruggs; Dara Freedman; Haley Zapal; John Pizzuro; Jamin and Kiowa Winans; Robert Muratore; Laura Love; Dr. Sujit Sharma; Detective Rich Wistocki; Dr. Free Hess; Dr. Carl Marci; Chris McKenna; Nicki Reisberg; Amy Fandrei; Sophie Thompson;

Lauren Patrick; Steve Chamberlain; Karen Houghton; Gordon Neufeld, PhD; Gabor Maté, MD; Stephen Porges, PhD; Dee Wagner, LPC; Caroline Gebhardt, LPC; LeeAnne Terry; Amy Spangler; IBCLC; Dr. Christine Blume; Molly Walker; Dale and Dana McIntyre; Dr. James Andrews; Wade Beacham; John Walsh; Nancy Grace; Don Barden; Rob MacLane; Randy Hatcher; Mike Ellwood; Dr. Sharat Vallurupalli; Hillside Inc.; Sam Chapman; Marc Berkman; Ed Peisner; Tessa Stuckey; Shelley Delayne; NCMEC; NCOSE; Dawn Hawkins; Tom Dinse; Ben Tracy; Rob Stearns; Nancy Joffre; Howard and Suzanne; The Isenberg Family; Brooke Shannon; Kristen A. Jenson; Paige Dees; Mia Ljungberg Nevado; Dr. Darria Long Gillespie; Kim Wimpsett; Sanjay Varadharajan; Satish Gowrishankar; Katey McPherson; Leslie Rogers; Marissa Pilgreen; Michele Joyce; Paul Bahr; Rania Mankarious; Brynn-Marie Kloster; Alex Radu; Allison Scovell; Dayna Thompson; Rachael D'Addezio; Aniko Hill; my colleagues both in and outside of Bark Technologies; and everyone who has ever asked me to come speak to their group, large or small.

A sincere and heartfelt thank you to everyone above.

About the Author

Titania Jordan is the chief marketing officer and chief parent officer at Bark Technologies, where she leads efforts to keep more than 7 million children safer online and in real life. A nationally recognized voice on digital parenting, Titania regularly appears on shows like the *TODAY Show*, *Good Morning America*, Fox News, and CNBC. She's also been featured in the *New York Times*, *Forbes*, *Parents*, and the *Wall Street Journal*.

Before Bark, Titania hosted NBC Atlanta's *Atlanta Tech Edge* and advised brands like Apple, Nikon, and Samsung to help them market to women. With a passion for working at the intersection of parenting and technology, she has become a trusted expert in helping families navigate the challenges of the digital age. Her insights were also featured in the powerful documentary *Childhood 2.0*, which explores the staggering impact of technology on today's youth.

Titania co-authored the bestselling *Parenting in a Tech World* in 2020 and founded a thriving online parenting community with more than 550,000 members in 2017 by that same name.

When she's not advocating for safer digital spaces, you'll find her hiking, painting, or building epic LEGO cities with her family.

Connect with her and learn more: **TitaniaJordan.com**.

Index